SIMPLE OBJECT LESSONS FOR CHILDREN

TOM A. & MARTIE BILLER

BAKER BOOK HOUSE
Grand Rapids, Michigan 49506

ISBN: 0-8010-0793-3

Seventh printing, July 1988

Copyright 1980
by Baker Book House Company

Printed in the United States of America

Preface

Having served as youth ministers in four churches over the past years, we have seen many children slip away from the church. Though they were brought each Sunday by the bus ministry or by their parents, during adolescence they began to drift from the church. This alarmed us and tore desperately at our hearts. We wanted strong, involved, Christ-centered teenagers. We hungered, along with many godly pastors, to see our children both participate and feel needed within the church structure. We began to realize that many caring Christians needed literature to help them reach children in the church or in their homes.

This book has been prepared with the involvement of the child in mind. He must be an integral part of the church, not a brushed-off, "get away, you bother me" child but a precious soul of value to the Lord's work. In our own experience, we have seen loving pastors reach out with concrete illustrations, bringing many children into a right relationship with Jesus Christ. We witnessed the importance of establishing rapport even before the child becomes old enough to participate in the youth group. So we started establishing trust, beginning at the preschool levels. Parents, too, need to establish rapport with their children. Communication must begin at an early age because it becomes more difficult if put off.

Because life's pressures limit your time, we have given this book a very simple format. Be sure you spend time in prayer

5

before beginning each session. Ask God to guide, direct, and give you the words which *He* would have you speak. Pray over the needs and concerns of each child, reassuring him/her of your love, and of God's unfailing love.

We have found it necessary for children to relate to something concrete and tangible. Because Bible sermons are often abstract, it is difficult for children to pay attention. Since a child's attention span is so short, the sermon often does not reach him. The child may see his Sunday school time as an activity time, not as a time in which to make a commitment to Jesus Christ. The children may want to be a part of the "big church," and we must reach them on *their level* in "big church," too. Jesus said, "But suffer the little children to come unto me," not just, "Suffer the little children." Let us not allow our children to "suffer" in the home devotional or church service by having to sit still and listen for long periods of time to something that is over their heads. Let us encourage them to find Christianity an active and practical life-long blessing.

You will find many benefits in establishing a junior sermon within your church service or your family devotional.

1. The junior-sermon concept establishes a direct interest in the children. Children are quick to pick up on that loving concern. What joy is felt when we know that others are preparing something especially for us! It is a very positive reinforcer.

2. You should see regular attendance increase when you use the junior-sermon concept. Children like for grownups to see them come up to the front. We all like to be on parade once in a while.

3. The child becomes an important part, not just a subculture, of the church (and home). The children find the church and home to be for them, as well as for the adults.

4. You will see that not only will the attendance of the children increase, but also the adult attendance will increase. Children interested in the junior sermon will compel their parents to come to church. Usually, Christian parents will be more apt to come if they know their child has a part in the service. The par-

ents and children therefore become "involved" in the church. They see the church as an active, vital part of their lives.

5. A much-needed relationship is established between pastor (or parent) and the child. Often children see the pastor as a distant figure too saintly to approach. The junior-sermon concept can help the pastor establish himself as a "friend" with his congregation. The pastor (or parent) can be seen as a fun-loving and interesting person. He is caring for each person in his church (or family).

6. This book will establish the sense of human belonging to our Father God. God loves us so much that He provides messages even in the simplest things.

7. The object lessons will provide a concrete truth to which we can relate. We can easily remember a live baby chick, and that can cue the Bible truth to focus in our minds. This is a stimulus memory prod.

8. The object lesson creates a further conversation between parent and child after the service or family devotional. The child may have questions for the parent to answer, or the parent may follow up with a question for the child to answer.

We are sure you will find many other benefits to this system. But the most important benefit is the salvation of the child, and perhaps of the parent, too.

Here are some tips in setting up this program. These object lessons are simple. You may adapt them for any age level by beefing them up or watering them down. Remember to speak on the age level of the child. Don't feel silly. You must make an effort to simplify your adult vocabulary. Be creative, expand, contract, or even delete, if you desire.

After using several of these object lessons you will be able to create your own lessons. Be aware of objects around you which could be used as a theme. Mostly, we have chosen items in our house and designed the lesson around them. You do not need to spend a great deal of money in the production of these lessons. Use the items around you. Don't buy anything unless absolutely necessary.

You may borrow from your neighbors. This will give you an opportunity to witness to them while you are borrowing. Imagine the wonderful witness you can have while answering the question, "What in the world are you going to do with this in your devotional?"

Decide who is going to give the lesson. It could be the pastor or the youth minister, or a deacon or layman. Even a variety of these people would work. For the family devotional, we recommend the father as teacher.

Decide where you are going to use the object lesson: an adult church service, junior church, Bible school, camp, evening service, a puppet ministry, or home devotional. The junior-sermon concept is adaptable to all of the above ministries, but we have found it especially meaningful in the morning adult worship service.

Decide what age level you want to reach. The preschool and elementary school child is exceptionally receptive. However, for variety, you may want to call the teen group to come forward some Sunday, or even the senior citizens. Be flexible!

Be prepared. Always prepare several Sundays ahead. Children are spontaneous and frank. You can never depend on them to give the exact answer you want. You should guide them at this point. Never reject an answer, just help the child to see where he is wrong without condemning. Since you can't program the answer into the children, you must be flexible. The Lord gives us the words to say when we allow direction from the Holy Spirit. Even when you think the lesson is going completely sour, the Lord will bring truth out of it. Be prepared to laugh at yourself. Be prepared to say, "I don't know," to some of the curious questions. The one thing you can learn to depend on in these object lessons is that you can't depend on anything (except the Lord)! But you will grow and learn and even be taught by the children.

We ask the children to come to the front of the church for the object lesson. You will need to prepare chairs or reserve pews. Even a clean floor will work. In the home devotional, it is easy to sit around the table. But it is essential to also vary the situations at home. At home you may encourage your children to choose the place where they want to have the object lesson. Involvement means including the child.

We have used Scripture texts for most lessons, and we find the Scripture essential. The children need to relate the concept to Scripture. *Without Scripture, children do not know what God says about a specific topic.* You probably will find many other applicable Scriptures to substitute if you desire.

We have also included familiar songs and choruses. If you cannot sing, have a helper lead the singing. Please do not make this complicated or polished. This singing needs to be a joyful noise unto the Lord, not a prerecorded message.

This book is easily adaptable for a puppet ministry. Puppets can do the summary as a dialogue. This can be done behind an upright piano, a piano enclosure, movable partitions, or even a hand-held curtain. Puppets can speak directly to the children or to the leader in a Kukla, Fran, and Ollie type exchange.

These object lessons need not be used in any specific order. They may be used when they specifically apply to your sermon topic or relate to your home environment.

Families will find this object lesson book adds needed spice to their family devotionals. Often family devotionals get in a repetitious rut, but this book will be a great aid in preventing stagnation.

We sincerely hope you will find this book of great benefit. You are reaching tomorrow's church. With care and attention, tomorrow's church will be stronger. Your love and guidance will be used of the Lord. You are a shepherd, with the responsibility of leading others to Christ.

Tom and Martie Biller
Dayton, Tennessee

Contents

1
Mix It Right

Materials: Egg beater, spoon, electric mixer

Scripture: *"How blessed is the man who does not walk in the counsel of the wicked, nor stand in the path of sinners, nor sit in the seat of scoffers!"* (Ps. 1:1, NASB).

"There are 'friends' who pretend to be friends, but there is a friend who sticks closer than a brother" (Prov. 18:24, LB).

See the things I brought today? Each week I bring something special, and today I have a mixer, a spoon, and an egg beater. What are these things used for? (*To blend things together.*) Yes, to mix things.

Often it is good to stir or blend things together. But there are some things that should never mix. For example, a Christian should never choose bad friends to run around with.

Listen to what the Bible says in Psalm 1:1 (NASB): "Blessed is the man who does not walk in the counsel of the wicked, nor stand in the path of sinners, nor sit in the seat of scoffers." God does expect us to live in this world, but He does not want our *best* friends to be sinners.

Proverbs 18:24 (LB) says, "There are 'friends' who pretend to be friends, but there is a friend who sticks closer than a brother." Who do you think that friend is who sticks closer than a brother? (*Allow answers.*) Yes, God is the one who sticks closer than a brother. We should choose Him as our dearest friend and then be wise about the other friends we choose.

2

Dada, Mama

Materials: Jars of baby food, baby cereal, baby bottle

Scripture: *"Then we will no longer be like children, forever changing our minds about what we believe because someone has told us something different, or has cleverly lied to us and made the lie sound like the truth. Instead, we will lovingly follow the truth at all times—speaking truly, dealing truly, living truly"* (Eph. 4:14, 15, LB).

"As newborn babes, desire the sincere milk of the word, that ye may grow thereby. If so be ye have tasted that the Lord is gracious" (I Peter 2:2, 3, KJV).

Is anyone here hungry today? Let's see, I have some food to share with you. (*Pull jar of baby food and other baby items out of bag.*)

What's the matter? Don't you like this food? Oh, it's baby food. Don't you eat baby food? (*No.*) Why not? (*We are too big and grown-up.*)

Your Christian life is like that, too! When you start your Christian life, you learn the basics in the Bible. Then, as you grow and mature as a Christian, you understand bigger ideas. It's important to "eat," or study, the Bible. God feeds you through His Word.

Let's see what God says about this matter in I Peter 2:2, 3 (KJV). (*Read.*) God doesn't want us to stay baby Christians and to be pushed around in our ideas. Ephesians 4:14, 15 says that God wants us to grow so we won't be fooled by clever people who want to lead us away from Christ. God wants us to grow up to be truthful in our speech, dealings, and in all life situations. Let's make a real effort to study and grow in God's will.

3
The Mouse Trap

Materials: A new mouse trap and a pencil, unsharpened, with which to trip the trap

Scripture: *"He keeps you from all evil, and preserves your life. He keeps his eye upon you as you come and go, and always guards you"* (Ps. 121:7, 8, LB).

We come in contact with the traps of sin every day. We can be caught if we are not protected.

(*Hold up the mouse trap.*) Boys and girls, what is this? (*Wait for their responses.*)

Yes, that is right. It is a mouse trap. What does a mouse trap do? (*Pause.*) It snaps little mice that get too close to it.

To lure the unwanted house guest to the trap, cheese is placed right here (*point*). This is the trigger. Let's set the trap. Watch out! It can hurt you. (*Snap the trap with the pencil.*) Now, I can pick up the trap and handle it; the trap is safe since it has been snapped.

Sin is like this trap (*reset trap*). We, as little mice, can be trapped if we get too close to sin. The only way we can escape the sin trap is if God goes before us (*snap the reset trap*) and takes the snap out of the trap.

(*Read Psalm 121:7, 8, LB.*) If we pray for help, God will guide us and keep us from the sin trap. Remember, when you see a sin trap you must not touch it. If you do, you may be hurt. Also, remember that God can keep you from being hurt by sin. It is wonderful to have a caring God who preserves us. He wants to protect you. He keeps His eye on you as you come and go. He *always* protects you. What love!

Let's pray and thank the Lord for His love and protection. (*Close in prayer.*)

4

Caution, Busy Street Ahead!

Materials: Make large traffic signs: Stop, Yield, Slow, Right Turn Only, Left Turn, Caution, Railroad Crossing.

Scripture: *"Children, be obedient to your parents in all things, for this is well-pleasing to the Lord"* (Col. 3:20, NASB).

"Honor your father and mother. This is the first of God's Ten Commandments that ends with a promise" (Eph. 6:2, LB).

I need several helpers today to hold up these signs. (*Choose children to come forward and help.*) Let's hold the signs up high.

The rest of you pretend that you are driving a car.

What would you do if you came to the first sign? (*Stop.*) Yes, you'd put your foot on the brake and stop.

Now, if you came to a yield sign, you would wait to see if a car was coming and let it pass first, before you proceeded. If you needed to turn right, you would get in the "Right Turn Only." And for this sign (*point to left turn sign*) you would turn left. For this sign (*point to caution*) you would proceed with caution. Finally, for the railroad crossing sign, you would slow down or stop at the crossing and look both ways before going.

These signs are important. If your parents didn't obey them, what would happen? (*There would be a lot of accidents.*) Yes, people would get hurt.

Your parents are like these signs. God gave you parents to guide you and give you advice. If you don't obey them, then you could hurt others and yourself—just like being in a wreck.

God is pleased when you obey your parents. (*Read Colossians 3:20, NASB.*) God has placed your parents over you. They are responsible to the Lord for you. (*Read Ephesians 6:2, LB.*) Parents aren't always right, but God commands you to obey them. You must remember to please the Lord by obeying, even when you feel your parents are wrong. Keep trusting the Lord and He will work things out the right way.

5

Turn on Route 1

Materials: A globe, a road map

Scripture: *"A highway will be there, a roadway, and it will be called the Highway of Holiness"* (Isa. 35:8, NASB).

"Because strait is the gate, and narrow is the way, which leadeth unto life, and few there be that find it" (Matt. 7:14, KJV).

Do you know that some day we are all going on a trip? In fact, I even brought a map along to help us find the way. Will someone hold this map up for me? (*Choose someone to help hold the map. Then pretend to try to find the correct road, but be unable to find it.*) Wow, I can't find the right road. It's hard to read this complicated road map.

Let's see if I can find it on this globe. (*Hold up globe and pretend to look.*) It's hard to find your way sometimes. Often people add so many numbers and routes on the map that you can't find your way.

It's that way with salvation, too. Men try to make it difficult to find Christ, but God made the road straight and narrow. You need to ask God to forgive your sins and come into your heart as Lord and Savior. You then become a child of God and are on the right road to heaven. (*Read Isaiah 35:8, NASB; and Matthew 7:14, KJV.*)

Don't allow any man, no matter how smart he is, to attach any extra requirements for salvation. The way to salvation is free and simple, and that is why it is difficult for people to accept it. People always want to be the smartest and to add on their ideas. So follow God's Word, and pray to receive Christ today. Then you will be ready for your trip.

6

Pennies from Heaven

Materials: Piggy bank, checkbook, money, tithe envelope

Scripture: *"Bring all the tithes into the storehouse so that there will be food enough in my Temple; if you do, I will open up the windows of heaven for you and pour out a blessing so great you won't have room enough to take it in"* (Mal. 3:10, LB).

"Every one must make up his own mind as to how much he should give. Don't force anyone to give more than he really wants to, for cheerful givers are the ones God prizes" (II Cor. 9:7, LB).

Here is a piggy bank. What do you do with it? (*Save money.*) Here is a checkbook. What is in it? (*Money.*) I also brought money and a tithe envelope. Today we are going to talk about giving our money to the Lord.

It is important to start giving to the Lord even when you are small. If the Lord has blessed you with money, then you should share with others by giving to the Lord. Malachi 3:10 says that our tithes should be used to help others. If you share your money, then God will pour out a blessing from heaven on you. (*Read Malachi 3:10, LB.*)

It is very important that you give with the attitude of happiness and love. Otherwise you will not receive a blessing from your tithe. The word *tithe* means tenth. No one should tell you how much to give, but you should give according to your love of God. (*Read II Corinthians 9:7, LB.*) We are to be cheerful givers. So when you use this tithe envelope, the gift inside will be your gift of happiness. You have shared from your blessings with others.

7

God Gives Full Measure

Materials: Measuring spoons, measuring cups, measuring tape, and a ruler (put in a sack)

Scripture: *"For if you give, you will get! Your gift will return to you in full and overflowing measure, pressed down, shaken together to make room for more, and running over. Whatever measure you use to give—large or small—will be used to measure what is given back to you."* (Luke 6:38, LB).

The verse we are going to read today is one of my favorites, so we will get to it very soon. But first I want you to pull items out of this sack. (*Choose children to pick things out of the sack.*)

What are these? (*Pull first item out of sack.*) And what are these? (*Hold up second item.*) Can you tell me what this is? (*Hold up third item.*) And finally, what is this? (*Hold up fourth item.*) All of these items have something in common; do you know what it is? (*They are all used for measuring.*)

Measuring is important, isn't it? Have you ever been told you can have as much candy as you can hold in one hand? You try to pack as much candy as possible into your hand, right?

God gives us blessings in that way, too. He says He packs blessings for us in overflowing measure. If we give to the Lord, then we will get in return. We can never outgive the Lord. He just gives and gives.

Listen to this wonderful verse in Luke 6:38 (LB). (*Read*) The Lord will give you more than full measure, based on how generously and happily you give to Him. So give of your time, talents, and money to God, and you will be fully blessed.

8

Bread for My Life

Materials: Hot dog bun, hamburger bun, and a loaf of bread

Scripture: *"They replied, You must show us more miracles if you want us to believe you are the Messiah. Give us free bread every day, like our fathers had while they journeyed through the wilderness! As the scriptures say, 'Moses gave them bread from heaven.'"*

"Jesus said, 'Moses didn't give it to them. My Father did. And now he offers you true Bread from heaven. The true Bread is a Person—the one sent by God from heaven, and he gives life to the world.'

"'Sir,' they said, 'give us that bread every day of our lives!'

"Jesus replied, 'I am the Bread of Life. No one coming to me will ever be hungry again'" (John 6:30-35, LB).

I brought some bread with me today. Who would like a taste? (*Allow for raised hands, then pinch off small bits of bread for a taste.*) I thought that was pretty tasty.

Way back in Bible times, bread was one of the most important parts of the meal, just as it is today. In fact, the people asked Jesus for more bread, just after He had fed them. Listen to what they said. (*Read John 6:30-35, LB.*)

Did they really need bread like the kind you just tasted? (*No.*) These people really needed spiritual bread. They needed to accept Christ as their Savior. They needed to believe in Christ as the Messiah, the Son of God. At once these people realized that Christ was the true Bread, sent from God the Father to provide for them a way of forgiveness and a place in heaven. They knew that their search for truth was over. Jesus filled their hungry feeling to find God.

Each day when you eat bread, remember that Jesus is the only One who will satisfy your need for salvation. He fills your needs.

9

Copy Cat

Materials: People dressed in clothes from different time periods, e.g., a person dressed in full skirt, bobbie socks, saddle shoes, and a ponytail for the 1950s; a person in a mini-skirt for the 1960s; another in a halter dress from the 1970s. (These are just examples; they need not be rigidly followed.) Put decade label around the model's neck.

Scripture: *"Don't copy the behavior and customs of this world, but be a new and different person with a fresh newness in all you do and think. Then you will learn from your own experience how his ways will really satisfy you"* (Rom. 12:2, LB).

I have a fashion show for you today. We will see Miss 1950 first. (*Allow model to stand in front and show off dress style.*) Next, let's see Miss 1960. (*Allow model to come forward.*) Finally, let's see Miss 1970. (*Allow third model to come forward. Then ask all three to leave before finishing your observation.*)

You saw the dress styles. What did you think? (*Have a short discussion.*) Each style was very different. The Lord expects Christians to be different too—not different by trying to keep up with every new fad, but by experiencing how to be unique as a Christian. (*Read Romans 12:2, LB.*) God wants us to learn when to draw the line—when we should not go along with everything the world has to offer. This is not only true in dress styles, but also in honesty at school, and in how we treat our parents. We must be different in all these ways, too.

Always ask yourself if you are acting the best way you can to show others you are a Christian. Try to be a good example—one that your friends will want to copy.

10

Ring Out for Christ

Materials: Two bells—one large, one small. Remove clapper from large bell. Bells should be lined up in front of the children so that they can see, but not touch.

Scripture: *"Fight on for God. Hold tightly to the eternal life which God has given you, and which you have confessed with such a ringing confession before many witnesses"* (I Tim. 6:12, LB).

Hi, kids! Today I have two objects setting up here on this table. What are they? (*Bells.*) What do you use bells for? (*Allow for answers such as a bell for fire, school bell, music bells, door bell, etc.*) Many bells like the telephone and doorbell call us. Also, bells warn us as, for example, does a burglar alarm.

Jesus tells us we are like bells. We call out to others about Jesus. Listen while I read this verse. (*Read I Timothy 6:12, LB.*) Jesus tells us to ring out about Him before many people. Did you ever think of yourself as a bell for Jesus? Well, let's try ringing the bells I have on this table. Which one do you think will be loudest? (*The large one.*) (*Choose two children to ring the bells, the small bell first, then the large one.*)

What happened to the large bell? (*It didn't ring.*) Why not? (*There is nothing inside.*)

So you see, to be able to ring out or tell about Jesus, you must have something on the inside. You must have Jesus inside as your Savior to be a witness for Him, or else you will be hollow like this large bell. Remember, you can be a small bell (child) and still carry the message that Jesus saves.

11

Who Are You?

Materials: Celery in a clear glass filled with water to which has been added several drops of red food coloring. Allow to set overnight.

Scripture: *"And I pray that Christ will be more and more at home in your hearts, living within you as you trust in him. May your roots go down deep into the soil of God's marvelous love; and may you be able to feel and understand, as all God's children should, how long, how wide, how deep, and how high his love really is"* (Eph. 3:17-18, LB).

Look at this celery. I put it in a glass filled with water and red food coloring. What happened to the celery? (*It absorbed the red food coloring.*)

Do you realize that we are like this celery? We absorb and become like the things around us. What does that mean? If we choose naughty friends, what happens to us? (*We are apt to become naughty.*) If we are around people who cheat? (*We learn to cheat.*) If we are around caring people? (*We learn to care for others.*) What if we surround ourselves with things of the Lord? (*We become Christ-like.*)

Listen to Ephesians 3:17-18 (LB). (*Read.*) These verses say for us to put our roots down into Christ, and then we will become more Christ-like. We will learn how long, how wide, how deep, and how high God's love is.

Stretch your arms to show "how long," stretch your arms to show "how wide," stretch your arms to show "how deep," and stretch your arms to show "how high" God's love is. God loves you. It is great to be loved and to choose the right people to have around us.

12
Really Corny

Materials: An ear of corn (count the kernels on this ear of corn and record the number), and one kernel of corn.

Scripture: *"That you may walk in a manner worthy of the Lord, to please him in all respects, bearing fruit in every good work and increasing in the knowledge of God"* (Col. 1:10, NASB).

Guess what! A miracle happened in my garden! I planted one single kernel of corn in the earth and watered it (*hold up kernel*), and a stalk of corn grew. On that stalk were four ears of corn. I brought one of the ears with me today. (*Hold up ear of corn.*) Just look how many individual kernels of corn there are on this ear, and all I planted was *one* kernel. How many kernels do you think there are on this ear of corn? (*Allow for guesses.*) There are _____ (*insert number*) kernels on this one ear. Just think! One planted kernel of corn produced _____ (*insert number*) kernels. This pleases me to see such a great harvest.

God wants us to produce good works for Him, too. God sows the seed of salvation in our hearts. Then we are to produce good works. What are some good works we can produce? (*Allow for answers such as, caring for others, praying, tithing, being honest, being obedient, etc.*) Another good work we can produce is other new Christians. We can lead people to Christ. Can you see how this cycle grows? You help another person to receive Christ, and he leads others to Christ. The others then reach even more people for the Lord. Just like this one kernel, we can produce much more fruit.

13

Tree Rings

Materials: A cross-section piece from a tree to show the rings of growth.

Scripture: *"And I pray that Christ will be more and more at home in your hearts, living within you as you trust in him. May your roots go down deep into the soil of God's marvelous love; and may you be able to feel and understand, as all God's children should, how long, how wide, how deep, and how high his love really is; and to experience this love for yourselves, though it is so great that you will never see the end of it or fully know or understand it. And so at last you will be filled up with God himself"* (Eph. 3:17-19, LB).

Let's list some of the kinds of trees we know about. There are oak trees, cherry trees, peach trees, maple trees, spruce trees, orange trees, plum trees, poplar trees, dogwood trees, magnolia trees, and walnut trees. Wow, we haven't named anywhere near the number of trees known in our town. There are still a bunch more, aren't there?

Did you know that trees grow a little each season? The most growth is in the spring and summer. Then the tree rests in the fall and winter. Here, look at this cross-section from the inside of a tree. (*Display the cross-section.*) Do you see all the rings? If we could count each ring, we would know the age of this tree.

We must grow in Christ step by step, too. Christ wants us to know Him, and to know His love. (*Read Ephesians 3:17-19, LB.*) These verses tell us to grow and put our roots down into Christ. We want to find out how long, how wide, how deep, and how high God's love is. We will see that God's love for us is never ending.

Song: *Deep and wide, deep and wide;*
There's a fountain flowing deep and wide.
Deep and wide, deep and wide;
There's a fountain flowing deep and wide.

14

Trumpet Blast

Materials: A person who can play a trumpet call from the back of the church or from some *hidden* place

Scripture: *"Just as the lightning comes from the east, and flashes even to the west, so shall the coming of the Son of Man be"* (Matt. 24:27, NASB).

". . . they shall see the Son of man coming in the clouds of heaven with power and great glory" (Matt. 24:30, KJV).

"So be prepared, for you don't know what day your Lord is coming" (Matt. 24:42, LB).

"For the Lord Himself will descend from heaven with a shout, with the voice of the archangel, and with the trumpet of God . . ." (I Thess. 4:16, NASB).

Today we are going to talk about Jesus returning to earth. When Jesus was born on earth, we celebrated Christmas. Later He died on the cross to provide forgiveness for our sin, and He ascended into heaven. That is why we celebrate Easter and Ascension Day. Jesus left us with the promise that some day He will come back to earth for us. We will be taken to heaven with Him. First, the dead Christians will rise to meet the Lord, and then the living Christians will follow.

There will be some signs for us to look for to know when Jesus is coming. The Bible says we will not know the exact day when Jesus is coming. (*Read Matthew 24:42, LB.*) And Jesus will return as quick as lightning. (*Read Matthew 24:27, NASB.*) We will *see* Him unmistakably when He comes. (*Read Matthew 24:30, KJV.*) And, also there will be a loud trumpet blast when Jesus comes for us. (*Read I Thessalonians 4:16, NASB.*) (*Then have the trumpeter play a loud herald.*) Do you hear that? I arranged for him to play, but what if that was really Jesus coming back for His own? Would you be ready for Jesus to come today? Have you invited Jesus into your heart?

If you don't know Jesus as your Savior, then you should pray to receive Him today. Then you will be prepared for His return. Jesus will come to take *you* to heaven with Him!

15

Time Marches On

Materials: Egg timer, stop watch, alarm clock, wall clock, a metronome, or any kind of time instrument

Scripture: *"There is an appointed time for everything. And there is a time for every event under heaven"* (Eccles. 3:1, NASB).

"We can rejoice, too, when we run into problems and trials for we know that they are good for us— they help us learn to be patient. And patience develops strength of character in us and helps us trust God more each time we use it until finally our hope and faith are strong and steady" (Rom. 5:3-4, LB).

"You need to keep on patiently doing God's will if you want him to do for you all that he has promised" (Heb. 10:36, LB).

"For when your patience is finally in full bloom, then you will be ready for anything, strong in character, full and complete" (James 1:4b, LB).

What is something you really want, but don't have yet? (*Allow answers such as, "I want a bike"; "I want to go to Disney World"; etc.*) It's hard to wait for something you really crave. I brought all these instruments to help us tell time. (*Demonstrate each instrument and what it is used for.*)

How often has your mom said, "Just be patient, we'll get to go swimming later"? Patience is happily waiting for something. (*Read Romans 5:3-4, LB; Hebrews 10:36, LB; and James 1:4b, LB.*) God says that learning to be patient is good for us. We can't expect everything we want immediately. We must learn to wait on God's perfect timing. (*Hold up clock.*) God has a set time for everything to happen, according to His plan. (*Read Ecclesiastes 3:1, NASB.*) We must trust God fully, because we know He has a perfect plan for each one of His children.

16

Don't Be Lonely

Materials: A bunch of weeds

Scripture: *"There are 'friends' who pretend to be friends, but there is a friend who sticks closer than a brother"* (Prov. 18:24, LB).

"I will never, never fail you nor forsake you" (Heb. 13:5, LB).

I heard a love story the other day. A boy wanted to show his girl how much he loved her by giving her gifts. One day he came with candy. The next day he took her to a fine restaurant. And the third day he brought her flowers.

Now, look what I have here (*show the weeds*). Do you think that boy would have pleased his girl with these weeds? (*No.*) Well, even though we try, sometimes we can't always feel happy with our friends. Somehow, they always disappoint us, just as the weeds would have disappointed the girl friend. Sometimes we feel lonely or upset by our friends.

But Jesus says that when you feel lonely you should remember that He is always with you. (*Read Hebrews 13:5, LB.*) And when friends disappoint you, remember that Christ is your friend, no matter what. He loves you all the time and will always stick with you. (*Read Proverbs 18:24, LB.*) God really loves you and cares about you. When you get down, remember these verses. Go back and read them; they will help.

17

Knock Down and Get Up

Materials: Building blocks

Scripture: *"Humble yourselves in the sight of God, and he shall lift you up"* (James 4:10, KJV).

I brought some blocks with me today. I think blocks are really fun to play with. I used to work hard just to see how high I could stack them. Have you ever done that? (*Yes.*) Let's work together and stack some of these blocks. (*Let each child stack a block.*) See, we did a pretty good job!

Sometimes my brother would come in the room where I was playing with the blocks. Guess what he did when he saw the blocks stacked so high. (*Kicked them or knocked them over.*) Right! It used to make me so disappointed to have him knock them down. Did that ever happen to you?

Satan is like that too. We work hard to try to be like Jesus. We do nice things like hold our tempers (*place a block*) or tell the truth (*stack another block on top*) or obey our teacher (*place another block on top*), and when Satan sees us trying to grow more like Christ—guess what Satan tries to do? (*Satan tries to knock us down.*) Yes, Satan tries to knock us down. And sometimes he succeeds. But we have to pick ourselves up and try again, because God promises to lift us up and help us.

Let's read James 4:10. It says, "Humble yourselves in the sight of God, and he shall lift you up." All we have to do is ask God for help, and He will pick us up and help us. It's good to know that Satan can't keep us down. When Satan tries to make us do bad things, God is there to pick us up after we fail and He will set us on the right road again. So trust God—He will always pick us up.

47

18

Satan Uses Decoys

Materials: Duck decoys and duck call

Scripture: *"And Jesus answering them began to say, Take heed lest any man deceive you: For many shall come in my name, saying, I am Christ; and shall deceive many"* (Mark 13:5-6, KJV).

"And he said, Take heed that ye be not deceived: for many shall come in my name, saying, I am Christ; and the time draweth near: go ye not therefore after them" (Luke 21:8, KJV).

How many of you have ever been hunting? (*Allow for response.*) I used to go duck hunting with my dad in the fall. We would get up very early and sneak out to the pond. We would tie a string to these things. What are they? (*Duck decoys.*) Then we would go back to a hiding spot called a duck blind to wait for the real ducks. When the real ducks flew over, it was my job to jiggle the string to the decoys so that they would look like real ducks swimming around. Dad would blow the duck call, and the real ducks would come flying down to take a look around. Do you know what happened when the real ducks flew in? (*You shot the real ducks.*) Right! Bang! Bang! Then we would have something for dinner.

Satan often works like a duck decoy and a duck call. Satan tries to fool us. Sometimes he makes something seem so right—like when we pretend we are sick so we can stay home from church. Or Satan will tell us it's okay if we just try drugs. Or Satan makes us feel embarrassed to witness for Jesus. Satan also likes to pretend he is Jesus, so he can fool people into serving him.

Listen to these verses (*Read Mark 13:5-6, KJV; and Luke 21:8, KJV*). Here we see that Satan is going to use people to try to pretend they are Christ. But we will know when Christ really is here on earth. Because when Christ comes, there will be a loud trumpet sound, and His coming will be like lightning coming from the east shining unto the west (Matt. 24:27). Don't even listen to men who say they are Christ, because when the real Christ comes you will definitely hear and see Him; no one will have to come and tell you! You will hear and see His coming.

19
Float On

Materials: A life preserver or life jacket

Scripture: *"As far as the east is from the west, so far has He removed our transgressions from us"* (Ps. 103:12, NASB).

"Yet now God declares us 'not guilty' of offending him if we trust in Jesus Christ, who in his kindness freely takes away our sins" (Rom. 3:24, LB).

I went boating the other day. My friend, who went with me, insisted I wear this thing! (*Hold up the life jacket.*) Why do you suppose he wanted me to wear this? (*To keep you from drowning.*) Well, the life jacket would help me float if an accident happened.

That made me think: some people get weighed down by their sins. Even though God will forgive their sins when they ask, sometimes people don't forgive themselves.

After you do something wrong, ask God to forgive you. Then God declares you "not guilty" of those sins any more. (*Read Romans 3:24, LB.*) Don't keep blaming yourself and putting yourself down. Keep afloat and learn from that experience. God has removed your sin. (*Read Psalm 103:12, NASB.*)

20

The Lamb

Materials: Picture of a lamb, or a stuffed or ceramic lamb

Scripture: *"And if he bring a lamb for a sin offering, he shall bring it a female without blemish. And he shall lay his hand on the head of the sin offering, and slay it for a sin offering in the place where they kill the burnt offering. And the priest shall take of the blood of the sin offering with his finger, and put it upon the horns of the altar of burnt offering, and shall pour out all the blood thereof at the bottom of the altar: And he shall take away all the fat thereof, as the fat of the lamb is taken away from the sacrifice of the peace offerings: and the priest shall burn them upon the altar, according to the offering made by fire unto the Lord: and the priest shall make an atonement for his sin that he hath committed, and it shall be forgiven him"* (Lev. 4:32-35, KJV).

"Again the next day after John stood, and two of his disciples; and looking upon Jesus as he walked, he saith, Behold the Lamb of God!" (John 1:35-36, KJV).

Do you know how the Lord forgives your sins? First you ask Jesus into your heart as Savior, then, whenever you sin, you can pray and ask forgiveness, and God will forgive you. Jesus died on the cross and His blood washes away our sins when we ask Him into our hearts. That is why the Bible calls Him the "Lamb of God." (*Read John 1:35-36, KJV.*)

Do you know how people were forgiven of their sins before Jesus came on earth? In Leviticus 4:32-35 it says they took a pure female lamb and killed her. They took the blood to the altar and sprinkled it, then burned the rest of the lamb.

Could you take a lamb and kill it? (*No.*) God provided an easier way. God gave His Son Jesus to be killed once for us. This act forgives our sins when we ask Christ to be our Savior. That is why Jesus is called the "Lamb of God."

21

Persecution

Materials: Oars to row with

Scripture: *". . . the Lord your God fights for you, just as he has promised"* (Josh. 23:10, LB).

"Blessed are they which are persecuted for righteousness' sake: for their's is the kingdom of heaven" (Matt. 5:10, KJV).

Have you ever heard this song? (*Sing "Row, Row, Row Your Boat."*) This song says to row *gently* down the stream. It isn't always easy to row a boat, because sometimes you have to row upstream against the current. That's why I brought these big oars. (*Show oars.*) I'm going to have to work hard.

Living as a Christian in today's world is like rowing upstream. We have to be different and act different, too, so people will know we are kind, loving, and true to God's Word. Some people will try to give us a difficult time, but God says, "Blessed are they which are persecuted for righteousness' sake: for their's is the kingdom of heaven." As we stand up for Jesus, we are blessed. Don't ever get discouraged for Jesus is always with you. (*Read Joshua 23:10, LB.*) Jesus promises to stick with you through thick and thin.

Let's sing "Row, Row, Row Your Boat" again. This time it will mean more for us; it will mean sticking up for Jesus every day.

22

Egg Trinity

Materials: Poster as shown, raw egg, clear glass bowl

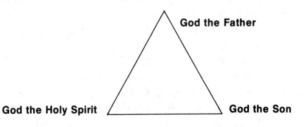

Scripture: *"You love him even though you have never seen him; though not seeing him, you trust him; and even now you are happy with the inexpressible joy that comes from heaven itself. And your further reward for trusting him will be the salvation of your souls"* (I Peter 1:8-9, LB).

Look at the poster I have. Read it with me: *God the Father, God the Son, God the Holy Spirit.* This is called the *Trinity.* Say it: *Trinity.* Trinity means three in one. There are three separate distinct parts to one God, just like this egg. Look at it. It's one egg, but has three parts: the shell, the white, and the yolk. (*Crack the raw egg into a clear glass bowl.*) All three parts are important, and all three parts make up one egg. The Trinity is something like this egg: God the Father, God the Son, and God the Holy Spirit work together to make up God. Say the Trinity with me again. (*God the Father, God the Son, God the Holy Spirit.*) Each part is God and each part has a special job. Remember, this is called the Trinity. (*Read I Peter 1:8-9, LB.*)

23

On Display

Materials: Magnifying glass, microscope

Scripture: *"Commit everything you do to the Lord. Trust him to help you do it and he will"* (Ps. 37:5, LB).

". . . overwhelming victory is ours through Christ who loved us enough to die for us" (Rom. 8:37, LB).

There are many things I can't do very well. I can't sing or play the piano or ski or paint or fix my car or get straight As in school or make the football team or play tennis or skate. As you can see, my list could go on forever.

Do you ever feel like this—like you just can't do anything? Or maybe you feel you are not really *great* at anything. You feel like everyone is looking at you—examining how well you do. It's like using these. (*Show the magnifying glass and microscope.*) What are these used for? (*To get a better look at something.*) Sometimes we feel like we are under a magnifying glass or a microscope. It is not a very comfortable feeling.

But God says that if you work hard to prepare yourself, He will help you, too. (*Read Psalm 37:5, LB.*) When you face a tough situation prepare yourself and then trust that God will be with you to help you. Don't put yourself down like I did at the beginning of the lesson; try to do things to the very best of your ability, and God will honor you. (*Read Romans 8:37, LB.*)

24

Make a Good Name for Yourself

Materials: Name tags; a roll of tape to attach the name tags to each child; a marking pen to write each child's name on his tag

Scripture: *"If you must choose, take a good name rather than great riches; for to be held in loving esteem is better than silver and gold"* (Prov. 22:1, LB).

I am glad we could all gather here today. We are going to talk about names. I brought tags to write your names on. Let's do this. (*Pass out the tags, then go around and write each child's name.*) Now look at your name on the tag. Your parents took time to choose that name especially for you. You have the job to make your name represent something good, so that when people talk about you, they will talk with respect. If we keep our reputation good, then we will be a good representative of God. (*Read Proverbs 22:1, LB.*) God says our good name is worth more than silver and gold. Protect your good name by always being honest and upright. (*Finish by passing out tape and attaching name tags to each child.*)

25

Cleaned Up

Materials: K2R spot remover and a rag to wipe with, paint remover, nail polish remover. Use each product on a sample spot.

Scripture: *"And I will cleanse away all their sins against me, and pardon them"* (Jer. 33:8, LB).

"But if we are living in the light of God's presence, just as Christ does, then we have wonderful fellowship and joy with each other, and the blood of Jesus his Son cleanses us from every sin" (I John 1:7, LB).

"But if we confess our sins to him, he can be depended on to forgive us and to cleanse us from every wrong" (I John 1:9, LB).

We are going to do an experiment today. I brought some cleaners with me today, and we are going to remove some stains. First, we will use the K2R, since it has to dry and be brushed off. (*Spray on the sample spot you have brought.*) Then let's try this paint remover on this piece of wood, which has a little paint on it. Did it come off? (*Allow answer.*) Also, we will try taking some nail polish off. (*Work on a prearranged helper.*) All of these products are cleaners.

Did you know that Jesus is a cleaner, too? Jesus cleans the sin in our life. His blood washes away our sins when we ask Him to be our Savior. (*Read I John 1:9, LB; and Jeremiah 33:8, LB.*) Yes, Christ is our cleanser. Let's go back and see if the K2R cleaned out this spot. (*Brush away the K2R and look at the spot.*) Each time you wash off a spot, think of the sins you need to confess to Jesus. Then Jesus will cleanse you from those spots of sin.

26

Heal Me, Please!

Materials: Several people painted with large red dots to look like measles

Scripture: *"I will give you back your health again and heal your wounds" [God is talking to Israel here]* (Jer. 30:17a, LB).

"And their prayer; if offered in faith, will heal him, for the Lord will make him well; and if his sickness was caused by some sin, the Lord will forgive him. Admit your faults to one another and pray for each other so that you may be healed" (James 5:15-16, LB).

Health is important. Many people take vitamins to be healthy. Some people go to health clubs to exercise and they stay fit. Health is important. How many of you have ever been sick? (*Allow hands to be raised.*) What kind of sicknesses have you had? (*Allow a few answers, but watch this, as it could get very time consuming.*)

Let's look at these healthy people I have with me today. (*Call in your painted measles victims.*) Wow, something is wrong with these folks! Boy, what's wrong? (*They have the measles.*) They had better go home to rest! God will take care of us when we are sick. Listen to these verses. (*Read James 5:15-16, LB; and Jeremiah 30:17a, LB.*) We must pray for one another when there is sickness. Prayer is important in God's healing of us. We should also ask for forgiveness of our sins, so that sin won't keep us from being healed. Remember to pray for one another during illness.

27

A New Song in My Heart

Materials: Arrange ahead of time for the choir to sing "Amazing Grace," the pianist to play "Count Your Many Blessings," and the organist to play "It Is Well with My Soul" or any favorite songs from the hymnal, as long as there are three different songs at the same time.

Scripture: *"He has given me a new song to sing, of praises to our God. Now many will hear of the glorious things he did for me, and stand in awe before the Lord, and put their trust in him"* (Ps. 40:3, LB).

Today you are going to have to use your ears. So take your fingers, and let's unplug our ears and get them ready. (*Do the motions of this.*) Let's listen to the choir sing a little of "Amazing Grace." (*Choir sings one verse or one line.*) Did you like that? It was beautiful wasn't it? Let's hear our pianist play a little of "Count Your Many Blessings." (*She plays.*) Boy, I really love that song, don't you? Okay, finally let's listen to our organist play, "It Is Well with My Soul." (*Organist plays a little.*) Those are my favorite songs. I like each of them equally well.

If I like those songs so much one at a time, I bet I'll like them three times as much if they are played all at the same time. (*All performers play and sing different songs at once.*) Oh, dear, that didn't sound like I thought it would. Did you like it? (*No.*) Why? (*Because they were all jumbled and none of them made sense.*)

God has a lesson in this for us. (*Read Psalm 40:3, LB.*) God wants us to be clear about what we are saying about Him. It is important that the songs we sing or the witnessing we do bring glory, not confusion, to Him. Whenever you do anything for God, prepare it carefully ahead of time, and pray for God's direction and help. That way, the things you do will help others clearly and easily find Jesus as Savior.

28

It Was No Picnic!

Materials: Picnic basket, thermos, picnic tablecloth

Scripture: *"And when he had given thanks, he brake it [the bread], and said, Take, eat: this is my body, which is broken for you: this do in remembrance of me. After the same manner also he took the cup, when he had supped, saying, This cup is the new testament in my blood: this do ye, as oft as you drink it, in remembrance of me. For as often as ye eat this bread and drink this cup, ye do show forth the Lord's death till he come"* (I Cor. 11:24-26, KJV).

It's a beautiful day. Let's go on a picnic. I brought a lunch (*hold up basket*) and something to drink (*hold up thermos*). Let me spread this tablecloth down here on the floor for you all to sit around. (*Invite the children to sit on the floor around the cloth.*)

Do you know the Lord and His disciples often had supper together? Probably they talked and had a good time together. Perhaps some days they had a picnic. But there was one day when Jesus and His disciples had dinner together that was *no* picnic. It's called the Last Supper; this was one of the times that Jesus told His disciples that He was going to have to die for the sins of the world. Jesus became our way for forgiveness of sins. This supper took place just before He was crucified on the cross. Jesus told His disciples to meet together as often as they could to have this special supper together. That way they would remember why Jesus died on the cross. Today we still celebrate this supper and call it communion. It is a time in which we remember and thank Christ for dying for us.

29

Glow Little Glow Worm

Materials: A long string of Christmas lights and a place to plug them in

Scripture: *"For ye were sometimes darkness, but now are ye light in the Lord: walk as children of light"* (Eph. 5:8, KJV).

Did you ever think that before you were saved you were in darkness? Satan is the prince of darkness. Who is the King of Light? (*God.*) We know that Jesus is the light of the world. Jesus gives us His light when we ask Him to come into our hearts. So we have to light up this world of sin while we live here.

Christians should have a special glow of God shining through them, just like this string of Christmas lights I have brought. Come help me hold up this string of lights. (*Allow the children to stand in a line and hold up the lights.*) Now we will turn out the church lights to represent the sin in the world. (*Turn out sanctuary lights.*) See what happens to these tiny lights. They shine even brighter in the darkness. They stand out. You stand out and are special when you let your light shine for Jesus. Listen to this verse: (*Read Ephesians 5:8, KJV.*)

30

Make It Clear

Materials: Someone who can speak a little of a foreign language—German, French, or Spanish, etc.

Scripture: *"Yet in the church I had rather speak five words with my understanding, that by my voice I might teach others also, than ten thousand words in an unknown tongue"* (I Cor. 14:19, KJV).

Hi friends! Today, I brought a friend with me. I'd like you to meet him. This is Mr. _____; he is here for a visit. (*Allow Mr. _____ to speak in a foreign language.*) Hey, how come you aren't talking with Mr. _____? I wanted you to get to know him. Why aren't you sharing ideas? (*Because he is speaking a different language.*) What language do you think he is speaking? (*Allow for answers.*)

Would it work if I let Mr. _____ bring the sermon? (*No.*) Why not? (*We can't understand him.*) That's right, we can't understand him. If I had an interpreter it would be fine, wouldn't it? (*Sure.*)

In the same way, when we have a chance to witness about Jesus, we must be very clear. That way people will *know* what we are talking about. We must tell people that Jesus is the Son of God, who gave His life on the cross to wash away our sins. All we need to do is ask God to forgive our sins, and believe in Jesus, and accept Him as our Savior. This is clear and simple to understand. So be as clear as you can when you are witnessing.

31

I Am Drawn to Him

Materials: Vacuum cleaner and confetti or litter which the cleaner can pick up

Scripture: *"But the Helper, the Holy Spirit, whom the Father will send in My name, He will teach you all things, and bring to your remembrance all that I said to you"* (John 14:26, NASB).

You must think I'm planning to do some work around here (*point to vacuum*). Not really; I'm going to use this to show you a little about the Holy Spirit. You know that God is three in one— God the Father, God the Son (Jesus), and who else? (*God the Holy Spirit*.) The Holy Spirit has many jobs, one of which is to draw you close to God, or to point you toward God.

Your mom uses her vacuum to suck up pieces of litter off the floor. There is a drawing power because of the motor inside. Let's see if it works. (*Sweep up confetti; perhaps let a child try, too*.)

The Holy Spirit works like this, too. When you are a Christian, the Holy Spirit lives inside you and acts like this motor. He draws you toward God and toward remembering about God. Let's read John 14:26 (NASB). (*Read*.) When you think about God and are praising Him in your heart, remember that the Holy Spirit is always there to encourage you to do so.

32

Who's There?

Materials: Cabinet door (You can borrow one of these from a carpenter or a cabinet shop.)

Scripture: *"Ask, and it shall be given you; seek, and ye shall find; knock, and it shall be opened unto you: For everyone that asketh receiveth; and he that seeketh findeth; and to him that knocketh it shall be opened"* (Matt. 7:7-8, KJV).

"Behold, I stand at the door, and knock: if any man hear my voice, and open the door, I will come in to him, and will sup with him, and he with me" (Rev. 3:20, KJV).

Have you ever heard a knock-knock joke? Here's one: Knock, knock. (*Who's there?*) Orange. (*Orange who?*) Orange you glad you came today?

Knocking is an important action. It's one way people know you are at the door. Jesus says He is knocking at the door of your heart, just waiting for you to open the door and let Him in. (*Read Revelation 3:20, KJV.*)

Listen to this! (*Knock on the little cabinet door.*) God wants you to ask Jesus into your life to be your Savior. When you feel encouraged to go forward or to seek out someone to talk to about Christ, do it. What happens if I don't use a door? (*It sticks shut and won't open.*) If you don't open your heart's door, then the next time Jesus knocks it will be easier to turn Him down and not open the door. But *you* must do the opening. Jesus won't force you to open your door. When you do open your door, then Christ opens new areas of love and enjoyment. You can trust Him to guide your life. (*Read Matthew 7:7-8, KJV.*) Open your door to Christ today, won't you?

33

Power Source

Materials: Several flashlights, only one with batteries; and a book

Scripture: *"But the Lord said unto Samuel, Look not on his countenance, or on the height of his stature; because I have refused him: for the Lord seeth not as man seeth; for man looketh on the outward appearance, but the Lord looketh on the heart"* (I Sam. 16:7, KJV).

(*Hold up a book.*) Have you ever heard someone say, "You can't judge a book by its cover"? Do you know what that means? (*Allow for answers.*) Yes, it means the outside appearance won't always tell you what is inside.

I brought some flashlights with me today. Who would like to come up and hold a flashlight? (*Choose helpers.*) Hold the flashlights, but don't turn them on until I tell you. Which one of these flashlights do you think will shine the brightest? (*The children will probably pick the largest.*) Let's see if it is the brightest. Please turn your switches on. (*Only one flashlight will light.*) Why do you think this one flashlight works? (*It's the only one with batteries.*) Yes, it has batteries, a power source, inside.

This is true with Christians, too. There are nice, kind people who are not Christians because they have never accepted Christ. They do not have a power source inside. The only way your light can possibly shine for Christ is if you have asked Him into your heart as your Savior. Don't look on the nice appearance some people may display on the outside—look inside at their hearts. (*Read I Samuel 16:7, KJV.*)

34

Shining Light

Materials: Candle, matches, glass

Scripture: *"You are the world's light—a city on a hill, glowing in the night for all to see. Don't hide your light! Let it shine for all; let your good deeds glow for all to see, so that they will praise your heavenly Father"* (Matt. 5:14-16, LB).

God calls us the world's light. Do you know what that means? (*Allow for answers.*) We are to allow God's love to shine from us to light the world. We are to tell others how to find Jesus as their Savior. Let's demonstrate that by lighting this candle. (*Do this.*) In a very dark room, this candle can be a big help. In fact, before electricity, people read by fire light. So this candle was very important.

Do you know what would happen if I hid this candle under this glass jar and cut off the air supply? (*Allow answer.*) Yes, the light would get dim and go out. (*Do this experiment; practice it beforehand.*) It is important to keep your light shining; otherwise you will become a dim and weak Christian. Let's sing the chorus "This Little Light of Mine."

Song: *This little light of mine,*
I'm gonna let it shine.
This little light of mine,
I'm gonna let it shine,
Let it shine, let it shine, let it shine.

Hide it under a bushel? (No!)
I'm gonna let it shine.
Hide it under a bushel? (No!)
I'm gonna let it shine.
Let it shine, let it shine, let it shine.

You have an important mission in this world to share the light of God with others. (*Read Matthew 5:14-16, LB.*)

35

Push Me Over, Pull Me Up!

Materials: A sturdy box (wooden) to stand on

Scripture: *"Therefore, my beloved brethren, be ye steadfast, unmoveable, always abounding in the work of the Lord"* (I Cor. 15:58a, KJV).

"For I can do everything God asks me to, with the help of Christ who gives me the strength and power" (Phil. 4:13, LB).

(*Choose a fair-sized boy helper, not nearly as large as you.*) I need a boy to help me do a demonstration. (*Choose one.*) I want to show you that it is easy to be pulled down into sin by your non-Christian friends. I am going to stand on this box. I am the Christian. John is pretending to be the non-Christian, and he is going to try to push me off. Okay, John, push me off. (*Allow him to do this.*)

Now, that wasn't very difficult, was it? John easily knocked me, the Christian, down. Let's see if I can pull John up to my Christian level. (*Have John lie on the floor in front of the box you are standing on. Reach down and try to pull John off the floor.*) I can't pull John up. It is impossible. I am trying to point out that it is impossible to stay a strong Christian without the power of Christ behind us. It is easy to slide into sin. Only the strength and power of Christ can keep a Christian from falling and can pull a non-Christian out of sin. You cannot do it alone, in your own strength. You must call on the Lord and stay dependent on Him. Keep yourself in the middle of God's will and you will always be a useful Christian. (*Read I Corinthians 15:58a, KJV; and Philippians 4:13, LB.*)

36

Isn't Every American a Christian?

Materials: Plastic flowers arranged in a vase and a real plant for comparison

Scripture: *"Not all who sound religious are really godly people. They may refer to me as 'Lord,' but still won't get to heaven. For the decisive question is whether they obey my Father in heaven"* (Matt. 7:21, LB).

Take a look at these pretty flowers I have in this vase. Do you like them? Which color is your favorite? But there is something funny about these flowers. I have been watering them and nothing helps them grow. Can you tell me why? (*Because they are artificial.*) Well, they look very pretty and they fooled me. I thought they were real. But they never grew or produced any new baby flowers.

This is just like some people I know. They look and act like Christians, but they have never really asked Christ to come into their hearts and forgive their sins. I guess they are just pretending, like these artificial flowers. They say nice things, but they never take time to help others come to find Jesus as Savior. The artificial Christians are pretending, not living in Jesus.

But look at this little living plant. This is like a real Christian. It is rooted in soil. The soil a Christian is rooted in is Christ. The soil feeds the little plant and keeps it strong. Also, the soil encourages the little plant to produce new plants rooted in Christ.

Which plant would you rather be? I want you all to be living Christians. All you need to do is ask God to forgive your sins and come into your heart as Lord and Savior. If you haven't done this yet, you can do it today.

37

Special Delivery Gift: Especially for You!

Materials: One large wrapped box and lid with a big bow on it. Slips of paper written on as follows:

1. Matthew 7:11
2. James 1:17
3. love
4. joy
5. peace
6. patience

7. gentleness
8. goodness
9. faith
10. meekness
11. temperance

Scripture: *"If ye then, being evil, know how to give good gifts unto your children, how much more shall your Father which is in heaven give good things to them that ask him?"* (Matt. 7:11, KJV).

"Every good gift and every perfect gift is from above, and cometh down from the Father of lights, with whom is no variableness, neither shadow of turning" (James 1:17, KJV).

(Have a teenage boy, acting as delivery boy, bring the large package to you, saying: Special Delivery package for Mr. _____. Who will sign for this?)

You say: Right here, I am Mr. _____. I'll take it.

Wow, kids, look at this gift! Isn't it beautiful? What do you suppose it is? *(Allow for guesses; don't let them see inside.)* Let's open it and see what is inside. *(Open box.)* Here is a paper. I'll read it for you. *(Read Matthew 7:11 and James 1:17.)* Jesus loves us so much that He gives us gifts. God doesn't give us just toys and games, He gives us personality gifts, such as, *(have these printed on construction paper and pull out of gift box)* love, joy, peace, patience, gentleness, goodness, faith, meekness, and temperance. I would like some of you to come up and hold these pieces of paper and we will read the words together. *(Do this.)*

I am glad Jesus loves us. Do you know He gave us the best gift of all? He gave us His life for forgiveness of our sins. When you see a package like this, remember that Jesus gave you the gift of His life on the cross.

87

38

I Can't See You

Materials: Two balloons—one blown up, the other flat

Scripture: *"And I will pray the Father, and he shall give you another Comforter, that he may abide with you for ever; even the Spirit of truth; whom the world cannot receive, because it seeth him not, neither knoweth him: but ye know him; for he dwelleth with you and shall be in you"* (John 14:16-17, KJV).

"But the Comforter, which is the Holy Ghost, whom the Father will send in my name, he shall teach you all things, and bring all things to your remembrance, whatsoever I have said unto you" (John 14:26, KJV).

How many objects do I have with me today? (*Two.*) What are they? (*Balloons.*) Today we are going to talk about the Holy Spirit. He is part of the Trinity. Help me name the Trinity (*say together*): God the Father, God the Son, God the Holy Spirit. (*You may repeat several times for emphasis.*) The Holy Spirit is the third person in the Trinity.

I have never seen a picture of the Holy Spirit. I think the reason I have never seen a picture is because the Holy Spirit has not been seen. Instead, He lives in our hearts. He is the One who makes us want to accept Jesus as Savior. He is also the One who tells us not to steal. John 14:16-17 says we cannot see the Holy Spirit. (*Read the verses.*)

I guess the Holy Spirit acts sort of like these balloons. Look at this flat balloon. We are like that flat balloon before we accept Jesus and before the Holy Spirit comes to live inside us. We have no "go power." But when the Holy Spirit comes into our hearts, He fills us up, just as the invisible air inside this full balloon. The air helps the balloon float and bounce back; the Holy Spirit helps us overcome problems and He comforts us. That is why they call the Holy Spirit the Great Comforter.

Wasn't it kind of Jesus to send us the Holy Spirit to help in this world? When you accept Jesus, the Holy Spirit comes to help you. You can call on Him when you have problems. This week when something happens, either good or bad, you can ask the Holy Spirit to help you.

39

Jump on the Wagon

Materials: Several toy race cars and a board which can be propped up to race the cars down

Scripture: *"The good man does not escape all troubles—he has them too. But the Lord helps him in each and every one"* (Ps. 34:19, LB).

"The Lord is a strong fortress. The godly run to him and are safe" (Prov. 18:10, LB).

Have you ever watched car races on TV? They are very exciting, aren't they? But they can be dangerous, can't they? Those drivers spend years preparing to be racers. They hire special mechanics so their cars will be as fast and safe as possible. The drivers wear special fire suits and helmets to shield their bodies. If they would have an accident, they would be well protected. They make sure they are really prepared before they enter a race. We are protected in special ways by the Lord, too. Proverbs 18:10 says that God is a strong fortress. We aren't exempt from trouble, but God will help us through the trouble. (*Read Psalm 34:19, LB*.)

When you race cars at home, remember the care and protection God has for His children. Let's try a race here with the cars I brought. (*Pass out cars to helpers and then race them down the slanted board*.) Are you reminded by these cars that God protects you?

40

Where Are You, Lord?

Materials: Hair dryer or hair blower, electrical outlet

Scripture: ". . . this Jesus, who has been taken up from you into heaven, will come in just the same way as you have watched him go into heaven" (Acts 1:11, NASB).

"Behold, He is coming with the clouds, and every eye will see Him, even those who pierced Him" (Rev. 1:7, NASB).

Everyone place your hands in front of your nose. Now, breathe in and breathe out. What do you feel? (*Air coming out my nose.*) Now blow with your mouth. Can you see the air coming out your mouth? (*No.*)

I have a hair dryer with me, and I'm going to plug it in. Who would like to feel the air? (*Allow children to feel the air jet.*) We know that the air will come out our mouths when we blow, and air will come from the hair dryer, too. We also know that some day Jesus will be coming back to earth to receive us as His children. We don't know when He is coming for us. But we *will* see Him. It won't be like this hair dryer, which blows invisible air. We will actually see Him. Right now we aren't able to see Jesus because He is in heaven at the right hand of His Father. But the Bible says in Revelation 1:7 that all of us will see Him. (*Read Revelation 1:7, NASB.*) Since we know that Christ is coming for us, we should be prepared. We should be sure of our salvation and be witnesses to others who are without Christ.

41

Spice of Life

Materials: Cards with different spice names on them such as, cinnamon, thyme, pepper, salt, cloves, bay leaf, paprika, oregano, marjoram, and rosemary

Scripture: *"Ye are the salt of the earth: but if the salt have lost his savor, wherewith shall it be salted? It is thenceforth good for nothing, but to be cast out, and to be trodden under foot of men"* (Matt. 5:13, KJV).

I have some cards with words printed on them here in my hand. Let me pass them out to you. When I give you one, come and stand up here with me. (*Pass out cards.*) Let's see if we can read these together. Some of them are difficult words, but I will help you with them. (*Read.*) Cinnamon, thyme, pepper, salt, cloves, bay leaf, paprika, oregano, marjoram, and rosemary. Do you know what these are? (*Allow for various answers.*)

Mom can answer this for us. What are these words, Mom? (*Spices.*) Tell us, Mom, what do you think is the most important spice listed here. (*Salt.*) Yes, can you imagine corn on the cob without salt? Salt is so important. It brings out the flavor of everything. God calls us the "salt of the earth." We are to bring out the *best* in this earth. We can do that by living special, dedicated lives to Christ. That way we will win more people to a saving knowledge of Christ. We will be actively flavoring them with Jesus Christ. What an exciting mission!

42

Grow On

Materials: Different seeds glued on paper and labeled. Bend back the labels so they can't be read until revealed.

Scripture: *"But remember this—if you give little, you will get little. A farmer who plants just a few seeds will get only a small crop, but if he plants much, he will reap much"* (II Cor. 9:6, LB).

I brought some seeds with me today, and I want you to guess what they are. (*Hold up papers with seeds glued on, labels hidden so they can't be seen. Allow guesses and then show labels such as, corn, beans, watermelon, cucumber, tomato, peach, apple, etc.*)

Why do we plant seeds? (*To harvest a crop.*) Can we expect to get a large crop if we don't plant any seeds? (*No.*) We must plant a lot of seeds and nurture them to have a good crop. People are like that, too. We must plant seeds of witness about Christ to others before they are harvested and accept Christ into their hearts. (*Read II Corinthians 9:6, LB.*) Even though a person may not accept Christ the first time you witness to him, keep on praying and witnessing, because some day God may harvest his soul. You will get a blessing for helping to sow seeds of witness in others' hearts.

43

Where Is the Christian?

Materials: Three identical cups, a Ping-Pong ball and table

Scripture: *"Do not fear, for I am with you; do not anxiously look about you, for I am your God. I will strengthen you, surely I will help you, surely I will uphold you with My righteous right hand"* (Isa. 41:10, NASB).

"For God is at work within you, helping you want to obey him, and then helping you do what he wants" (Phil. 2:13, LB).

Have you ever played the game "The Hand Is Quicker Than the Eye"? I'm going to put this Ping-Pong ball under one of these cups. Now I'm going to scramble them really fast. Keep your eyes on the cup that has the ball under it. Which cup do you think the ball is under? (*Choose one child to guess. Do this several times.*)

Some Christians are like this little Ping-Pong ball. They try very hard to get lost in the crowd. They aren't brave enough to stand up for Christ. They receive Christ into their hearts, but get absorbed back into the world. God says for us not to be afraid to stand out for Him. (*Read Isaiah 41:10, NASB.*) Also, He says in Philippians 2:13 that He is at work within us. (*Read Philippians 2:13, LB.*) Don't get scrambled around or pushed into the corner by others. Christ is within you, so stand up for Him.

44

Totally You

Materials: Stamp ink pad, small pieces of paper for each child's thumbprint

Scripture: *"Thy hands have made me and fashioned me: give me understanding, that I may learn thy commandments"* (Ps. 119:73, KJV).

Do you know that you are a VIP? What does VIP mean? (*Allow for answers.*) VIP means "very important person." God made you a special individual. While each of you has a head, eyes, nose, and so on, God made you different from one another, too. I'm going to show you one way. Your fingerprints! (*Quickly take each child's thumbprint—you may want a helper.*) Each one of your fingerprints is different. Everyone in this church has a special set of fingerprints.

(*Read Psalm 119:73, KJV.*) "Thy hands have made me and fashioned me: give me understanding, that I may learn thy commandments." God made you special so that you could serve Him in many different ways. Just as there are many different fingerprints, there are many different ways for us to serve God. Each of us must strive to work the best way we can for God. Do that this week.

45

Muddy

Materials: A cardboard box with a crusty, muddy pair of boots inside

Scripture: *"Do not let sin control your puny body any longer, do not give in to its sinful desires. Do not let any part of your bodies become tools of wickedness, to be used for sinning; but give yourselves completely to God—every part of you—for you are back from death and you want to be tools in the hands of God, to be used for his good purposes. Sin need never again be your master, for now you are no longer tied to the law where sin enslaves you, but you are free under God's favor and mercy"* (Rom. 6:12-14, LB).

I put my boots in this cardboard box for a very good reason. I will hold the boots up. Tell me why I put them in the box. (*They are muddy*.) Yes, they are crusted over with mud. I didn't want to get the carpet soiled, so I put them in the box.

Have you ever walked in the mud? After you walk in the mud awhile, it gets very heavy on your shoes. It makes walking very difficult; it slows you down.

Sin is that way, too. We should always choose not to sin, because sin slows us down as Christians. It makes life difficult for us, just like this mud. (*Read Romans 6:12-14, LB.*) These verses explain to us that God wants to use us as tools, so we must clean sin out of our lives. We can do this through prayer and the power of the Holy Spirit. Don't trudge along drearily carrying sin. Keep yourself clean and useful.

46

The Big Squeeze

Materials: Sponge, paper towel, dish cloth

Scripture: *"Submit yourselves therefore to God. Resist the devil, and he will flee from you"*   (James 4:7, KJV).

I have three things here from my kitchen—a sponge, a paper towel, and a dish cloth. I use them all to soak up water. Let's see if they work. (*Choose three children to dab up a little water.*) Does the sponge soak up water? (*Yes.*) Does the paper towel soak up water? (*Yes.*) Does the dish cloth soak up water? (*Yes.*)

When we sit in church, we can soak up all the good ideas the pastor shares with us from the Bible. But we must squeeze ourselves a little each day to push out those ideas to other people. We need to share the "living water" within us.

We also need to be "squeezable" so that God can use us. It is difficult to use a hard, dried-up sponge. But when that same sponge is filled with water we can squeeze it into any shape. We need to submit ourselves unto God, and resist the devil, and he [the devil] will flee from us. That way, God can use us to tell others about Him.

47

My Pet

Materials: Pictures of different pets—cat, dog, canary, horse, etc.

Scripture: *"Even when walking through the dark valley of death I will not be afraid, for you are close beside me, guarding, guiding all the way"* (Ps. 23:4, LB).

"The Lord is near to the brokenhearted, and saves those who are crushed in spirit" (Ps. 34:18, NASB).

"Those who mourn are fortunate! for they shall be comforted" (Matt. 5:4, LB).

How many of you have a pet at home? (*Allow raised hands.*) Tell us what some of your pets are. (*Allow examples: cat, dog, bird, etc.*) Come up and hold these animal pictures.

We learn to love our pets so much, they become a real part of the family. They can even learn to do tricks to please us. If they get hurt or killed we are sad. We feel lonesome without them. We hurt when we lose our little friends. But even when we are sad, the Lord comforts us. Listen to these verses of comfort the Lord prepared for us. (*Read Psalm 23:4, LB; and Matthew 5:4, LB.*) The Lord has tender love for those who are brokenhearted. If you have ever lost a pet or a loved one, you know how loving God can be during these times. It also is important for us to comfort one another. If your friend has experienced a death in his family, then you should be especially loving to him. Remember to pray for one another in times of trouble.

48

A Good Workman

Materials: Tools: hammer, saw, screwdriver, etc.

Scripture: *"Study to show thyself approved unto God, a workman that needeth not to be ashamed, rightly dividing the word of truth"* (II Tim. 2:15, KJV).

I need to do a little repair work around here. Does anyone want to help me? (*Call up several children.*) We need to saw some wood first. Here, you saw this in half. (*Give the child the wrong tool, such as the hammer.*) Then we need to pound some nails. (*Give the child the wrong tool, such as the screwdriver.*) And we need to tighten some screws. (*Give the child the wrong tool, such as the saw.*)

Okay, get started! Hey, why aren't you working? (*The children will say they have the wrong tools.*) You're right, you can't hammer with a screwdriver, or saw with a hammer, or tighten screws with a saw, can you? (*No.*)

Jesus wants us to be prepared with the right tools to be the best Christians we can. Do you know how to get the right Christian tools? By studying! Listen to II Timothy 2:15. (*Read.*) To be the best workmen for Jesus, we need to study and memorize the Bible. When we *know* the Bible, then we can tell what is the truth or a lie. We can tell when someone is trying to teach us a wrong idea about God, or the wrong politics, or the wrong behavior. Knowing the Bible will help us to know the truth and not be fooled. The Bible is one of God's ways to talk to us. We can be the best prepared workmen by *knowing* and *studying* God's Word.

49

Which Way, Lord?

Materials: Compass, and/or a large picture of a compass (Make sure you know the directions while standing in your sanctuary.)

Scripture: *"As far as the east is from the west, so far hath he removed our transgressions from us"* (Ps. 103:12, KJV).

I need all of my helpers to stand up and assist me today. Okay, now everyone stand and make some room between you and the person beside you. Be sure you have some elbow room between you. What I want you to do is point to the direction I call out. For example, which way is north? (*Allow children to point without any assistance from you.*) Okay, now which way is south? (*Allow children to point.*) Which way is east, and which way is west? You have pointed out the direction, and I will correct you. (*Show the correct positions of north, south, east, and west.*) It was kind of hard to do that, wasn't it? We weren't sure which way the directions were.

God says he removes our sins as far as the east is from the west. (*Read Psalm 103:12 KJV.*) God takes our sins as far away as they possibly can be from us. Let's sing this chorus:

Song: *Gone, gone, gone, gone,*
Yes, my sins are gone.
Now I am forgiven;
In my heart's a song.
Buried in the deepest sea.
Yes, that's good enough for me.
I shall live eternally.
Praise God, my sins are G-O-N-E gone.

God will show you the right way to go. He will guide you.

50

Job Interview

Materials: Choose men and women ahead of time to tell a little bit about their jobs.

Scripture: *"The steps of good men are directed by the Lord. He delights in each step they take. If they fall it isn't fatal, for the Lord holds them with his hand"* (Ps. 37:23-24, LB).

"In everything you do, put God first, and he will direct you and crown your efforts with success" (Prov. 3:6, LB).

"And if you leave God's paths and go astray, you will hear a Voice behind you say, No, this is the way; walk here" (Isa. 30:21, LB).

Will the ladies and men who are going to help me, please come forward? Each of these people has a different job they are going to tell you about. (*Proceed to ask the name of the job and what they do.*)

It is good to have a job, to produce and help the world. God honors the job you do if you put Him first. (*Read Proverbs 3:6, LB.*) We know that Christians are directed by God in the jobs that they choose. God uses us in every area of work as His representatives. (*Read Psalm 37:23-24, LB.*) Even when we mess up, God picks us up and dusts us off. God sets us back on the right track. (*Read Isaiah 30:21, LB.*) It is wonderful to know that God is behind us and in front of us preparing the road ahead. We should serve Him to our fullest capacity. That means doing the best job we can possibly do.

51

Joy, Joy, Joy!

Materials: A cassette tape recorder with a tape of laughing

Scripture: *"For this day is holy unto our Lord: neither be ye sorry; for the joy of the Lord is your strength"* (Neh. 8:10b, KJV).

"For our heart shall rejoice in him, because we have trusted in his holy name" (Ps. 33:21, KJV).

"You have sorrow now, but I will see you again and then you will rejoice; and no one can rob you of that joy" (John 16:22, LB).

I want you to listen to this. (*Play the laughing tape.*) It is a tape of people laughing. How does it make you feel? (*Happy, silly.*) It is good to be happy, isn't it? And Christians have more to be happy about then anyone on earth. We have our sins forgiven, we know Jesus as our Savior, we have love overflowing from God and we will be in heaven some day. God tells us we should be happy, secure, joyous Christians. Listen to just a sample of the many verses where God tells us to be joyful Christians. (*Read Nehemiah 8:10b, KJV; Psalm 33:21, KJV; and John 16:22, LB.*) I like the way the last verse says that no one can rob us of the joy of God. Not even Satan can completely take away our joy. Let's sing that well-known chorus *"I've Got the Joy, Joy, Joy, Joy!"*

Song: *I've got the joy, joy, joy, joy,*
         Down in my heart.
               (where?)
         Down in my heart,
         Down in my heart,
         I've got the joy, joy, joy, joy,
         Down in my heart,
         Down in my heart to stay.

52

Out of Tune

Materials: A guitar out of tune and a guitar player who can show the children how to tune it

Scripture: *"He has given me a new song to sing, of praise to our God. Now many will hear of the glorious things he did for me, and stand in awe before the Lord, and put their trust in him"* (Ps. 40:3, LB).

I want to sing a song for you today. (*Begin singing "There's a New Song in My Heart Since the Savior Set Me Free" [or any other familiar song] with the untuned guitar.*)

Hey, wait a minute. This sounds awful. What's the problem? (*The guitar is out of tune.*) I need someone to tune this guitar. (*Call up guitar tuner to help.*)

Do you know that a non-Christian is like this untuned guitar? He is sour and sick with sin. He does not know Jesus. Jesus is like this guitar player. He can bring us into perfect pitch. He tunes us just right. When we become in tune with Christ, then we are in tune with everything. We can make harmonious, beautiful music. Christ gives us a new song. (*Read Psalm 40:3, LB.*) Now that this guitar is in tune, let's try this chorus again:

Song: *There's a new song in my heart,*
Since the Savior set me free.
There's a new song in my heart,
'Tis a heavenly harmony.
All my sins are washed away,
In the blood of Calvary.
Oh, what peace and joy,
Nothing can destroy.
There's a new song in my heart.

53

Quibble, Quarrel, Fight!

Materials: Arrange for two men to come in arguing about land ownership (or some other applicable subject), then allow the argument to accelerate into a fight, followed by a quick exit.

Scripture: *"He who is slow to anger is better than the mighty, and he who rules his spirit, than he who captures a city"* (Prov. 16:32, NASB).

"It is an honor for a man to stay out of a fight. Only fools insist on quarreling" (Prov. 20:3, LB).

Who is glad to be here today? (*Allow children to raise hands.*) I am excited to share with you today because (*allow the two men to interrupt your talk and begin the argument in front of the children*)— Wait a minute, guys. We're trying to have a Bible study here. Hold it! Don't fight! (*This is where the fist fighting should begin.*) Hey, take that outside! (*Help them out of the room.*)

Did you see that? What were they fighting about anyway? (*Allow answers.*) You know most fighting is over something little like this! And often people can never forgive after a fight. They carry a grudge for years. Listen to what God says about fighting. (*Read Proverbs 16:32, NASB; and Proverbs 20:3, LB.*) It is an honor to stay *out* of a fight; only fools insist on fussing. We should try to solve our problems in ways other than fighting. We also should be forgiving when others do us wrong. Otherwise, the fellowship of Christ will be hindered.

54

No More
Spankings

Materials: Paddle, hairbrush, belt, wooden spoon

Scripture: *"For the Lamb in the center of the throne shall be
their shepherd, and shall guide them to springs of
the water of life; and God shall wipe every tear
from their eyes"*   (Rev. 7:17, NASB).

*"He will wipe away all tears from their eyes, and
there shall be no more death, nor sorrow, nor
crying, nor pain. All of that has gone, forever"*   (Rev.
21:4, LB).

I want to show you some things that my dad used to use on me when I was naughty. Here is a paddle. Would you hold the paddle for me? (*Choose a helper.*) Here is a belt. Would you hold the belt? (*Choose another helper.*) Here is a hairbrush. Who will hold this? (*Choose a third helper.*) And finally, here is a wooden spoon. Would you hold this for me, please? (*Choose the fourth helper.*)

Look at these spanking machines. (*Have the helpers hold them up.*) They hurt, don't they?

We get spanked when we have been naughty and need to be taught a lesson. What are some reasons for getting spankings? (*Allow for answers.*) After you get a spanking, do you laugh? (*No.*) What do you do? (*Cry.*)

Do you know that when we get to heaven there will be no more crying? Even tiny babies will not cry. God will take all our tears away and replace them with joy and happiness. Listen to Revelation 7:17 (NASB). (*Read.*) This verse says that we will have Jesus as our Shepherd, and that God will take away our tears. Revelation 21:4 (LB) says God will take away death, sorrow, pain, and crying. All sadness will be gone forever. God wants us to be happy in heaven. We will be praising Him and rejoicing to be in heaven. What a wonderful God we have to love us so much as to provide us with such a happy place.

121

55

Misty

Materials: A pump spray bottle filled with water

Scripture: *"I've blotted out your sins; they are gone like the morning mist at noon! Oh, return to me, for I have paid the price to set you free"* (Isa. 44:22, LB).

How many of you have ever gotten up in the morning to see fog all around? You could barely see where you were going, the fog was so thick and soupy. It seemed like you were closed up in a tight box. Didn't it feel like the fog would never go away, and the day would be very dreary? But, amazingly enough, at noontime the sun came out and began to shine brightly. It was hard to remember that the morning started with such thick fog.

Our sins are like the fog to God. We start out with dark, nasty sins, just like the thick morning fog—sort of like this spray bottle. (*Squirt the mist bottle several times*.) God sent His Son Jesus to die on the cross to provide forgiveness of our sins. When we ask Jesus to be our Savior, He takes our sins and removes them as far as the east is from the west. How far is the east from the west? (*Allow for answers: The east is so far from the west that we can't measure*.) Those sins are never to be remembered again. (*Read Isaiah 44:22, LB*.) Our sins are gone like the morning mist. (*Squirt the spray bottle*.) Each time you see a spray bottle or the fog, think of how God forgives you.

56

Scared to Death

Materials: Rubber snake, plastic worms, and plastic spiders (Use pictures or drawings if necessary.)

Scripture: *"Fear not, for I am with you. Do not be dismayed. I am your God. I will strengthen you; I will help you; I will uphold you with my victorious right hand"* (Isa. 41:10, LB).

"Fear not, little flock; for it is your Father's good pleasure to give you the kingdom" (Luke 12:32, KJV).

I'm going to tell you a secret about myself. When I was eight years old, I was afraid of shadows. I would lie in my bed at night and sometimes I could see shadows of branches on my bedroom wall. It really scared me. I always thought someone was after me.

What are some other things that we could be afraid of? (*Allow children to list such things as, snakes, spiders, the dark, thunder, lightning, etc.*) Yes, there are lots of things we could be afraid of. In fact, I brought a few things with me that might be considered scary. Here is a snake. (*Pull out rubber snake.*) Here is a spider. (*Pull out plastic spider.*) And here are some worms. (*Hold up worms.*) These are awful, aren't they? But do you know that we don't *have* to be afraid. God is with us to protect us at all times, no matter where we are, even when we are alone in our own beds. God tells us to fear not. (*Read Isaiah 41:10, LB.*)

God has pleasure in giving us His kingdom, and part of that kingdom is feeling loved and protected and safe. (*Read Luke 12:32, KJV.*) When you are frightened, pray aloud to God. Talk to God and ask for comfort. He is always there to listen to you. God will comfort you. God does not want you to be foolish and to get yourself into dangerous situations when you should know better, but God will comfort your fears.

57

Worn Out

Materials: A rocking chair and lap blanket

Scripture: *"You will have courage because you will have hope. You will take your time, and rest in safety. You will lie down unafraid and many will look to you for help"* (Job 11:18-19, LB).

"Come unto me, all ye that labour and are heavy laden, and I will give you rest" (Matt. 11:28, KJV).

I believe I will get comfortable today. (*Pull up the rocker, and put on the lap blanket.*) I have worked hard this weekend. I scrubbed the floors, I mowed the lawn, I walked the dog, I washed the car, and did many other things. Would you like to make a big sigh with me? (*Lead the children in a big sigh.*)

Now tell me some of the work that you did. (*Allow for answers.*) I get very weary of all that work plus my job. I guess you get tired of all your chores plus your school work. But those things are very important.

Fortunately, God can help us with our burdens. When we get tired and depressed, we have the privilege of sharing our burdens with God through prayer. (*Read Matthew 11:28, KJV.*) God not only shares our burdens but provides answers for them. God gives us courage when we are weary. He helps us to depend on Him. (*Read Job 11:18-19, LB.*) It is wonderful to be able to relax, knowing that God is caring for us. Wow, I feel better and more rested already! (*Get up and stretch.*)

58

Flex Those Muscles

Materials: Weights, barbells, exercise equipment

Scripture: *"The Lord is their strength, and he is the saving strength of his anointed"* (Ps. 28:8, KJV).

"I can do all things through Him who strengthens me" (Phil. 4:13, NASB).

Let me feel your muscles. Each of you tighten your bicep muscles. (*Go around and feel the children's upper arm muscles.*) Strength is an important skill. You remember the story of Samson, don't you? He was a very strong servant of God as long as his hair was uncut. But when he told his secret of strength and his hair was cut, he became weak. In other words, he received his strength from God, and without God's favor he was nothing.

Who would like to try lifting these weights? (*Choose a few helpers to try this.*) Learning to be a weight lifter takes practice, training, and growth. You need training so you won't lift incorrectly and hurt yourself. You need practice so you can gradually build your muscles. And you need growth because a fifty-pound boy can't lift three hundred pounds. He must grow before he can attempt that much weight.

Your Christian life is similar to weight lifting. First, God is the source of your strength. Second, God trains you in His Word so you will be prepared. Third, you must practice and live your life to honor God. And fourth, you must grow in God to attempt larger and larger problems. (*Read Psalm 28:8, KJV: and Philippians 4:13, NASB.*) Remember, you are strengthened through the power of God, and the power of God is limitless!

59

Scrub, Scrub, Scrub

Materials: Toilet articles such as, soap, washcloth, towel, toothbrush, toothpaste, and shampoo.

Scripture: *"Come, let's talk this over! says the Lord; no matter how deep the stain of your sins, I can take it out and make you as clean as freshly fallen snow. Even if you are stained as red as crimson, I can make you white as wool!"* (Isa. 1:18, LB).

"There was a time when some of you were just like that [uncleansed] but now your sins are washed away, and you are set apart for God, and he has accepted you because of what the Lord Jesus Christ and the Spirit of our God have done for you" (I Cor. 6:11, LB).

In this bag I have some items from my bathroom. I'm going to call on you, and you can pick something out of the bag. Stand with me in the front and we will demonstrate what these items do. (*Allow several children to do this.*) Here is the toothpaste. What does it do? (*Cleans your teeth.*) Here is the soap. What does it do? (*Cleans your body.*) (*Repeat question and answer until all items are named.*) All these items clean us, don't they?

And Jesus cleans us from our sins. His death and resurrection washed away all our sins when we asked Him into our hearts to be our Savior. He washed away the sin of disobeying and stealing and cheating—all our sins. Listen to what the Bible says about Jesus cleaning our sins. (*Read Isaiah 1:18, LB, and I Corinthians 6:11, LB.*)

No matter how bad you think your sin is, Jesus can wash it away. All you need to do is pray and ask God to forgive you, and He will do it. He will make you as white as snow inside. That doesn't mean you will *never* sin again, but it does mean that you can always pray and ask God to forgive you. So when you jump in the bathtub to get your body clean, think about how clean you are on the inside. Maybe you need to talk things over with Jesus and ask Him to forgive you. Jesus never fails to do that! Isn't that great! Now you can be clean all the way through.

60

I'm All Wrapped Up

Materials: Blankets, warm coat, stocking cap

Scripture: *"And you say to him, 'Well, good-bye and God bless you; stay warm and eat hearty,' and then don't give him clothes or food, what good does that do? So you see, it isn't enough just to have faith. You must also do good to prove that you have it"* (James 2:16-17, LB).

Brrr! I have been cold all day long. I brought these warm clothes and blankets to wrap up in. Maybe now I can warm up.

Have you ever been where it is cold? (*Allow for answers.*) Sometimes I see people with just thin jackets on when it is cold. Some people don't have enough money to buy good warm clothes. Can you think of a way we could help them? (*By sharing our clothes or giving money to buy warm clothes.*) By being kind to others, they will be more willing to listen to you when you talk about Jesus loving and caring for them. It is important for Christians to do nice things for others. Listen to James 2:16-17. (*Read.*) It is our job to prove our love by helping out. So be aware! Look around you for special ways to help out.

61

He Holds Us Tight

Materials: Rubber boots, cleated shoes, hiking shoes

Scripture: *". . . unto him that is able to keep you from falling, and to present you faultless before the presence of his glory with exceeding joy"* (Jude 24, KJV).

Have you ever watched football? What kind of shoes do the players wear? (*Cleated shoes.*) Have you ever walked in the snow? What do you put over your shoes? (*Rubber boots.*) Have you ever seen mountain climbers? Or have you gone hiking? What kind of shoes should you wear? (*Hiking boots.*) Why do football players wear cleats? (*To get a good grip and keep from falling.*) Why do people wear these special kinds of boots in the snow? (*To keep from falling.*) Why do hikers wear these shoes? (*To keep from falling.*)

Jesus keeps us from falling, too. I don't mean falling like this. (*Fake a fall.*) I mean that Jesus keeps us from falling away from Him. Jesus wants us to stay in close fellowship with Him, because He is going to present us to His Father in heaven some day. Jude 24 says, "Unto him that is able to keep you from falling, and to present you faultless before the presence of his glory with exceeding joy!" Jesus wants you to stay close to Him by praying to Him, praising Him, and loving Him.

62

Give God a Hand!

Materials: Any object you can hold tightly in your hands, such as a scarf

Scripture: *"My Father, which gave them to me is greater than all; and no man is able to pluck them out of my Father's hand"*   (John 10:29, KJV).

I've been bad this week! I've been *so naughty*! My Dad would be ashamed of me if he knew what I did. Jesus is disappointed in me, too. But I can ask for forgiveness, and God will forgive me. I'm glad God doesn't throw me out of His family each time I do something naughty. He promises to hold on to me no matter what.

Let's demonstrate with this scarf. Here, try to pull it away. (*Allow a child to pull.*) I can hold on pretty tight, can't I? But God holds on tighter than anyone in the whole universe. God loves us so much that once we ask Him to be our Savior, He holds on and helps us forever. (*Read John 10:29, KJV.*) It's great to know God loves us that much, isn't it?

63

Fishers of Men

Materials: Fishing pole or net (*no* hooks for safety's sake.)

Scripture: *"Jesus called out, 'Come along with me and I will show you how to fish for the souls of men!'"* (Matt. 4:19, LB).

Has anyone here ever been fishing? (*Show of hands.*) Good! How many of you have ever caught a fish? (*Show of hands.*) Okay! I see that some of you haven't been fishing, so today we are going to show you a little bit about fishing. This is a fishing pole, and you cast the line out in the water and hope to catch some fish. (*Do this if you have room.*)

Jesus said in Matthew 4:19, "Come along with me and I will show you how to fish for the souls of men." He was sending His disciples out to fish for men, rather than fish.

Jesus wants each of us to go fishing with Him every day of our lives. We are to fish for people to bring to the Lord. We are to tell them how Jesus loved them so much that He died on the cross to forgive their sins. We must tell people how they can invite Jesus into their hearts to become their Savior. That way, we become fishers of men and helpers of Christ. Let's sing that chorus together:

Song: *I will make you fishers of men,*
Fishers of men,
fishers of men.
I will make you fishers of men,
If you follow me.
If you follow me, if you follow me;
I will make you fishers of men,
If you follow me.

I hope you will be good fishers each day!

139

64

Hair

Materials: Several wigs

Scripture: *"But even the very hairs of your head are all numbered. Fear not therefore: ye are of more value than many sparrows"*   (Luke 12:7, KJV).

"Let him have all your worries and care, for he is always thinking about you and watching everything that concerns you"   (I Peter 5:7, LB).

Did you ever hear that worrying makes your hair turn gray? Some people believe that is true, but I'm not sure how scientific that is! We all have worries, don't we? What are some of your worries? (*Worries about tests or fights with friends, etc.*)

Jesus says for us to tell Him our worries. (*Read I Peter 5:7, LB.*) He will help us with all our cares. It is good for us to have Jesus listen to our problems. He really cares about us! Do you want to know how *much* Jesus cares?

I need some helpers. (*Pick several kids to wear wigs.*) Put these on. (*Kids put on wigs.*) Who can guess how many hairs are in these wigs? You can't? Jesus not only knows how many hairs are on these wigs, but He knows exactly how many hairs are on each one of your heads. That's how much Jesus cares about you. You are *so precious* that He even has your hairs numbered (*Luke 12:7*). Aren't you glad you are so special?

65

I'm a Present

Materials: Ribbons cut in lengths to tie on each child's finger

Scripture: *"I beseech you therefore, brethren, by the mercies of God, that ye present your bodies a living sacrifice, holy, acceptable unto God, which is your reasonable service"* (Romans 12:1, KJV).

I want you to make yourselves presents to God. We know that God loves you and wants you to be His children. But you must ask Jesus into your hearts—present yourselves to Him. (*Read Romans 12:1, KJV.*)

Let's tie these ribbons on your fingers. Have the person beside you help. (*Allow the children to tie on the ribbons.*) When you look at these ribbons, I want you to think of yourselves as a special present to Jesus. If you haven't given your heart to Jesus yet, then today is the day to do it. Your heart and life is the best gift you can give to God.

66

Fan the Flames of Revival

Materials: A fan (fold-up) or a window fan

Scripture: *"Though I walk in the midst of trouble, thou wilt revive me: thou shalt stretch forth thine hand against the wrath of mine enemies, and thy right hand shall save me"* (Ps. 138:7, KJV).

Whew, it's hot in here. I guess I'll use this fan to cool off. A fan can be used for many things. It can cool off someone and it can even help start a fire.

Have you ever helped build a fire? What are some things you need to start a fire? (*Kindling, logs, matches.*) And you need to blow on the fire to help it to get hotter. I guess I could use this fan I have here.

If a person faints, you can use a fan to help revive him. God helps us to revive. When I get discouraged or depressed, or when I get in a rut, God revives me. Psalm 138:7 tells how God cares for me. (*Read.*) In a way, when I have trouble, God stretches out His hand and fans me. He revives me even in the middle of all my troubles. When Satan tries to tackle me hard and knock the wind out of me, God is right there to revive me, and He is always there to revive you, too.

67

All Gooped Up!

Materials: Several tempra paint colors, paint brush, and rinsing water

Scripture: *"There was a time when some of you were just like that [uncleansed] but now your sins are washed away, and you are set apart for God"* (I Cor. 6:11, LB).

"But if we confess our sins, he is faithful and just to forgive us our sins and cleanse us from all unrighteousness" (I John 1:9, KJV).

How many of you like to paint? Good! Do you like the colors I brought? I'm going to make a masterpiece for you right now. What color should I paint first? (*Dab on whatever color the children choose.*) Looks good. I think I'll use this one, too. (*Dab on another color without rinsing brush, so paint smears together.*)

Oh, no, something is going wrong and these colors are getting all goopy. Maybe I should put another color on. (*Dab on without rinsing again and smear them so it's a brown mess.*)

I did something wrong! I forgot to use this. (*Hold up rinsing water.*) What's this for? (*Rinsing the brushes.*) My picture would have been much better had I rinsed the brushes.

Our lives are like this, too. We need to clean the sin out of our lives each day by asking forgiveness each time we sin. God rinses us clean when we pray and ask forgiveness. Jesus washes us clean, just like the water washes the paint out of these brushes. And we start fresh again. If we happen to sin again, then we can pray again and ask forgiveness. We also must work hard to try not to sin if we can, but if we do, God is always there to wash us sparkling clean. (*Read I John 1:9, KJV; and I Corinthians 6:11, LB.*)

68

Who Would You Like To Be?

Materials: One poster of cut-out magazine pictures of girls, each picture numbered; one poster of magazine pictures of boys, each numbered

Scripture: *"He will swallow up death forever. The Lord God will wipe away all tears and take away forever all insults and mockery against his land and people. The Lord has spoken—he will surely do it"* (Isa. 25:8, LB).

Look at these picture posters I have made. Each picture is numbered. Examine these people's faces. Which person would you most like to be? Remember the face and the number, okay? Now I am going to find out which one you picked. (*Ask for their choices by number.*) Why did you like that face? (*It was handsome, pretty, smiling, smart looking, wealthy looking, healthy, etc.*)

Why didn't you choose this ugly person, or this girl crying? (*We don't want to be that way.*) No one wants to be unhappy or sickly, but, on earth, there are times when everyone goes through unhappy periods.

God says that there will be a day when we Christians won't have to suffer any longer. Death will have no power over us. No one can insult or mock us, and God will wipe away our tears. (*Read Isaiah 25:8, LB.*) Isn't it nice that we have a happy, peaceful existence to look forward to in heaven, and that God can comfort us right now through the Holy Spirit?

69

Who Is the Devil?

Materials: An easel, a large sheet of paper clamped to the easel, a marking pen, and a red crayon

Scripture: *"And no marvel; for Satan himself is changed into an angel of light"* (II Cor. 11:14, KJV).

"Be sober, be vigilant; because your adversary the devil, as a roaring lion, walketh about seeking whom he may devour" (I Peter 5:8, KJV).

I want you to describe for me what the world thinks Satan looks like. (*Lead the children in: red color, horns, tail, and pitch fork, etc.*) (*Sketch this image on the easel.*) This is what many people think Satan looks like. They think he will appear to them looking like this sketch. But Satan is clever. He can change his looks to appear in different forms. He was a serpent to Adam and Eve. He was once the most beautiful of all angels. The Bible says he walks about as a roaring lion. So, as you can see, Satan does not run around in a red suit like this sketch shows. He can change his appearance to trick you into sinning. Usually he tries to look as inviting as possible. He hopes this will lure you toward him and toward sin. Satan tries to make himself desirable, even though he is bad. So a sin often may look very appealing to you, but remember, it is wrong. Satan is hard at work trying to make you stumble. Look at him as he really is—a changing, very appealing trickster. Be careful! Put your faith in God. God provides Jesus and the Holy Spirit as protection for you.

70

Follow the Leader

Materials: None

Scripture: *"And a certain scribe came, and said unto him, Master, I will follow thee whithersoever thou goest."* (Matt. 8:19, KJV).

"If any man serve me, let him follow me; and where I am, there shall also my servant be: if any man serve me, him will my Father honour" (John 12:26, KJV).

How many of you have ever played "Simon Says"? It's an easy game. You do all the things Simon says you may do, but if Simon does *not* say that you may do something and you do it, then you are out. We will do a practice game so that you will catch on before we do a real game. (*Play a practice game, then do the real game, as time allows.*)

"Simon Says" is an easy game as long as you *follow*. Following is the key to success. If you don't follow, then you are out. It is like that with Christ, too. We need to follow Him and accept Him as Savior. If we do not follow Him, then we are out. Being out means we are on our way to hell. It is very important to follow Christ. (*Read John 12:26, KJV: and Matthew 8:19, KJV.*) When we follow Christ, we are also serving God, and God honors those who follow Christ. Whenever you play "Simon Says" think about your job of following Christ.

71

Mr. Big

Materials: Large adult size clothes

Scripture: *"As newborn babes, desire the sincere milk of the word, that ye may grow thereby"* (I Peter 2:2, KJV).

"But grow in spiritual strength and become better acquainted with our Lord and Savior, Jesus Christ. To him be all glory and splendid honor, both now and forevermore . . ." (II Peter 3:18, LB).

I brought some neat clothes with me today, and I'd like to have some of you model them for us. (*Pass out the clothes and have the children stand in front with them on.*) What's the matter? Why don't you like these clothes? I thought they were neat! (*They are all too big.*) You mean, you can't wear these clothes? (*No, we have to grow into them.*)

We have to grow in Christ, too. We don't start out being a "grownup" Christian. We become a Christian when we accept Christ as Savior, but we have to *grow* and *mature* to become more "Christ-like." We grow up in Christ by studying the Bible, praying, and attending church. II Peter 3:18 explains that we can grow in Christ by being better acquainted with Christ. (*Read.*) Soon you will grow into these big clothes. And if you feed on the Bible, you will soon grow up in Christ, too.

72

Step Up

Materials: Step ladder

Scripture: *"The path of the righteous is like the light of dawn, that shines brighter and brighter until the full day"*   (Prov. 4:18, NASB).

"For I am confident of this very thing, that he who began a good work in you will perfect it until the day of Christ Jesus"   (Phil. 1:6, NASB).

I brought a step ladder with me today. What does your family do with a step ladder? (*Allow for answers.*) A step ladder helps you stretch to reach up, doesn't it? Let me try that. (*Step on the first rung and reach up, then the second rung and reach up. But don't climb too high so you won't fall.*) Yes, I can reach higher each time.

Each day we should try to grow in Christ. We need to take steps to be closer to Christ. We can attend Sunday school and church to learn about Him, and also we can reach out to help others to be more Christ-like. Each day becomes a step closer to Christ. (*Read Proverbs 4:18, NASB.*) "The path of the righteous is like the light of dawn, that shines brighter and brighter until the full day." In reaching up toward God, we become a better person. Remember to step up for Christ.

73

Putty in His Hands

Materials: Different sizes of vases and pottery

Scripture: *"Go down to the shop where clay pots and jars are made and I will talk to you there. I did as he told me, and found the potter working at his wheel. But the jar that he was forming didn't turn out as he wished, so he kneaded it into a lump and started again"* (Jer. 18:2-6, LB).

I'd like to have a drink of tea. Which one of these pieces of pottery should I drink from? (*Cup*.) Yes, the cup seems to fit the need, doesn't it? Do you know how pottery is made? (*Allow for a child to tell, if one knows*.) Yes, a lump of clay is placed on a turntable and a potter shapes the clay into a vase or cup or plate.

We are like a lump of clay. Then as God shapes us and kneads us, we become an important piece of pottery. God can use us to do His work—just like this cup serves an important part in my life. (*Read Jeremiah 18:2-6, LB*.) When you feel God is wanting you to serve in a special way, God is molding you. Sometimes the molding is hard to take, especially if you aren't wanting to serve God. Sometimes God has to shape us over and over again until we become *willing* to do God's work.

74

Using Your
Good Sense

Materials: Touch—an object in a paper bag
Taste—a life saver
Smell—perfume
Sight—picture
Hearing—whistle

God gave us five senses. Do you know what our five senses are? (*Let the children name them.*) Yes, the five senses are touch, taste, smell, sight, and hearing.

What part of your body does *touch* have to do with? (*Hands.*) What part of your body does *taste* have to do with? (*Tongue.*) What part does *smell* have to do with? (*Nose.*) What part does *sight* have to do with? (*Eyes.*) What parts do *hearing* have to do with? (*Ears.*) All our parts are precious to God, and He wants us to use them in the best ways.

I have something in this paper bag. Who would like to feel it without looking and tell us what it is? (*Do this.*) I have something to taste. Who would like to tell us what flavor it is? (*Give a child a flavored life saver*) I have something to smell, who would like to tell us what it is? (*Do this.*) I have something to look at. What is it? (*Show picture.*) I have something to hear, who would like to listen and tell us what it is? (*Blow whistle.*) Most of us have the abilities to do all these things.

Sometimes we use our five senses in a *bad* way. For instance, we can allow our ears to listen to bad stories. Or, we could allow our tongue to say naughty words. We must be careful to honor God with our five senses. Let's sing this song together and maybe it will help us to keep our five senses busy on the Lord's side.

Song: *Oh, be careful little hands what you do.*
Oh, be careful little hands what you do.
For the Father up above is looking down in love.
So be careful little hands what you do.

Repeat each verse inserting: *tongue—say, eyes—see, ears—hear.*

75

The Teakettle

Materials: Teapot that whistles

Scripture: *". . . the joy of the Lord is your strength"* (Neh. 8:10, KJV).

Boys and girls, how do you act when you are happy? Yes, that's right, you want to jump up and down and get all excited. Let's sing a song about being excited about Jesus. (*Sing "Get All Excited" several times through.*) That song tells about how good it is to be excited for Jesus.

What is this? Yes, it's a teakettle which your mother uses to heat water for tea or coffee. What happens when the kettle gets hot? It begins to bubble. That's the way you feel inside when you are excited—kind of bubbly. When the water gets hot enough, it begins to make steam. The steam comes rushing out through the pour spout. This makes the kettle whistle. The kettle cannot hide its feelings. Whenever it gets excited, it whistles and tells everyone it's excited. Whenever we get all excited about Jesus Christ, we should bubble over and tell others about His love. Our Scripture verse tells us that our joy in the Lord is the strength of our life. (*Read.*) We should, therefore, share Jesus, the source of our happiness, with other people.

Song: *Get all excited, go tell everybody that Jesus Christ is King.*
Get all excited, go tell everybody that Jesus Christ is King.
Get all excited, go tell everybody that Jesus Christ is King.
Jesus Christ is still the King of kings.

Bill Gaither

76

Stick It to Them

Materials: Different size knives (butcher knife, carving knife, potato peeler, pocket knife) which you will display, then remove, or use pictures of knives.

Scripture: *"For the word of God is quick, and powerful, and sharper than any two-edged sword, piercing even to the dividing asunder of soul and spirit, and of the joints and marrow and is a discerner of the thoughts and intents of the heart"* (Heb. 4:12, KJV).

I brought some sharp instruments with me today, so only I will touch them. I have a butcher knife, which your mom might use to cut up a chicken. I have a carving knife with which your dad might carve a turkey. I have a potato peeler. I have a pocket knife, with which you might whittle a piece of wood. As you can see, there are many different types of knives. And they can be dangerous, if you don't handle them correctly.

God talks about the Bible as a sword. He says the Bible is swift and powerful. The Bible divides good from bad, and truth from a lie, just as a carving knife cuts meat apart. You can use the Bible as a help and protection from Satan's attacks. (*Read Ephesians 6:17, KJV.*) The Bible is the sword of the Spirit. It will be your guide and protector. So learn to use your Bible thoroughly. Turn to the Bible when you have questions. Become knowledgeable in the Word, and you will find it to be a great help.

77

Faded Out

Materials: Faded pair of jeans and a wilted flower

Scripture: *"The grass withers, the flowers fade, but the Word of our God shall stand forever"* (Isa. 40:8, LB).

How many of you own a pair of jeans? I want you to notice this pair of jeans. I've worn these jeans a lot. I wear them playing softball or working in the yard. When I first bought these jeans, the material was stiff and crisp. The color was darker blue. What happened to the dark blue color of my jeans? (*It faded as it got older.*) Yes, each time I washed them, the color faded. They just got worn out.

Now look at this flower. (*Hold up wilted flower.*) This flower used to look good and healthy, but something happened. What do you suppose happened to this poor flower? (*It faded or wilted.*) A lot of things that we own here on earth fade out. We trade in our cars, because they don't last forever. I'm sure you can think of many other things that don't last. But there is something that you can have that will last forever. That is having Christ as your Savior. Whatever we have from God is everlasting. (*Read Isaiah 40:8, LB.*) God's Word will last forever. So, dig into God's Word, the Bible, and memorize it. It is an everlasting gift from God.

78

Fruit Basket

Materials: A variety of fruit (apple, orange, melon, grapes, grapefruit, peach, banana)

Scripture: *"But when the Holy Spirit controls our lives he will produce this kind of fruit in us: love, joy, peace, patience, kindness, goodness, faithfulness, gentleness and self-control"* (Gal. 5:22-23, LB).

Today I brought some goodies with me. As I hold them up, you tell me what they are. (*Hold up each fruit and allow children to name it.*) These are all fruit, aren't they?

Have you ever watched a fruit tree grow? First, it starts with buds, then it blossoms, and finally the fruit appears.

This should be true in your Christian life, too. As you begin to grow and mature as a Christian, you bud, and as you read and study your Bible, you blossom. Finally, as you lead others to a saving knowledge of Christ, you have fruit. Other spiritual fruit is found in Galatians 5:22-23 (LB), which says, "But when the Holy Spirit controls our lives he will produce this kind of fruit in us: love, joy, peace, patience, kindness, goodness, faithfulness, gentleness, and self-control." Each time you see fruit in your lunch box or in the refrigerator, stop and think if your life is showing love, joy, peace, patience, kindness, goodness, faithfulness, gentleness, or self-control. Don't be a dead tree; be a budding, blossoming, fruitful tree.

79

Hello, Hello

Materials: Toy telephone

Scripture: *"Then, when you call, the Lord will answer: 'Yes, I am here,' he will quickly reply"* (Isa. 58:9a, LB).

(*Do a pretend conversation with your Dad.*) "Hello, Dad. How are you? Great! Listen, Dad, I'm so glad to talk to you. You always give me such good advice. I really appreciate you, Dad.

"I have this problem. I have a test in school tomorrow, and I'm nervous. What should I do? You say I should prepare myself the best I can? And have confidence in myself? Right! Okay, Dad. Thanks. I love you. Bye."

Did you listen carefully to that phone conversation? I was just talking to my dad. Prayer is a lot like conversation. We are just sharing with and talking to God. (*Give an example if you wish.*) We can tell God exactly the need we have, and perhaps ask forgiveness. Then we should thank God for the answers to our prayers. When we finish praying, we must listen for answers God has prepared for us. Remember, prayer does not have to be fancy words; it is just talking to God, an expression of what is in our hearts. (*Read Isaiah 58:9a, LB.*)

80

Ripples

Materials: Dishpan with water, several small pebbles (Practice this to see that the pebbles make waves, otherwise you need a larger pan.)

Scripture: *"Now go ahead and do as I tell you, for I will help you to speak well, and I will tell you what to say"* (Exod. 4:12, LB).

Gather around this table. I want to show you a little demonstration. (*Allow time for the children to gather around*.) I will describe the action, so the rest of the congregation can tell what is going on. I have a dishpan with water in it. Now watch; I'm going to drop a small pebble into it. What happened to the water? (*It rippled*.) (*Do this several times*.)

When we are living active lives as Christians, we should have an effect on things around us, just as this *small* pebble affects this water. We should be good examples of what Christ has done for us. People should be able to tell by our deeds we are Christians. Then our deeds will open doors for us to witness to others. Never be afraid to witness, because God will prepare words for you to say. (*Read Exodus 4:12, LB*.) Make a mark in this world for God. Be like this pebble and affect the people around you.

81

Watch Out for That Banana Peel!

Materials: Banana. Practice making a fake stumble and fall.

Scripture: *"I screamed, 'I'm slipping, Lord!' and he was kind and saved me"* (Ps. 94:18, LB).

"So, dear brothers, work hard to prove that you really are among those God has called and chosen, and then you will never stumble or fall away" (II Peter 1:10, LB).

(*Call children forward, then do your fake fall.*) Whoa, I really lost my balance. I just fell right down. How many of you have ever fallen? (*Raised hands.*) Have you ever seen a baby learn to walk? What happens? (*They fall a lot.*)

Look at this fruit! (*Hold up banana.*) What happens if you step on this peel? (*You will fall down.*) Everyone takes a fall now and then, even grownups.

We can take a spiritual fall, too. Sometimes we do things God doesn't like, such as cheating or telling lies. That is one way of falling away from God.

Even great Bible people such as David took a spiritual fall. Listen to what David said after his spiritual slip. (*Read Psalm 94:18, LB.*) "I screamed, 'I'm slipping, Lord!' and he was kind and saved me." So don't worry when you make a mistake. Start by asking God's forgiveness, then go on with your Christian life. Work hard at trying *not* to fall. (*Read II Peter 1:10, LB.*) That way you can live a steady, faithful Christian life.

82

Snore Not!

Materials: Blanket, pillow, robe, nightcap

Scripture: *"He will never let me stumble, slip or fall. For he is always watching, never sleeping. Jehovah himself is caring for you! He is your defender. He protects you day and night"* (Ps. 121:4-6, LB).

Boy, am I tired! I believe I'll take a little nap. (*Do this*.) Now, you each take care of yourself the best way you can.

Do you think this is the way God treats us? (*No*.) God always has time for us. God never sleeps or takes time out away from us. (*Read Psalm 121:4-6, LB*.) The Bible says God is our defender. Whenever you feel weak or alone, remember you can call on God at any time. Can I call for God's help at 2:00 a.m.? (*Yes*.) Can I call on God from a playground? (*Yes*.) Can I call on God when I'm weeping in my bed? (*Yes*.) I can trust God to always be there when I need His help. Remember, God never sleeps.

83

Eyeglasses

Materials: As many different types of glasses as you can get (sunglasses, bifocals, binoculars, monocle, etc.)

Scripture: *"Behold, the eye of the Lord is upon them that fear him, upon them that hope in his mercy. To deliver their soul from death, and keep them alive in famine"* (Ps. 33:18-19, KJV).

If you have trouble seeing things or reading, what do you do? You go to a doctor. He will examine your eyes and find out why you can't see well. The doctor may tell you that you need glasses. Glasses are used to correct eyesight problems people have.

Often we have difficulty seeing what God wants us to see. He has a specific way we are supposed to live. This means seeing our life through Christ's eyes. If we go to Christ in prayer, He will act as our eye doctor and help us see clearly. (*Ask one or more of the children to try on a pair of glasses.*) Can you see better or worse with these glasses? (*Allow answers; hopefully the vision will be worse.*) These glasses are not right for you. In your life with God, He knows just what to give you so you can see clearly how to follow Him. Your spiritual prescription for good vision is the Bible. God's holy Word lets you see clearly what He wants you to do. (*Read Psalm 33:18-19, KJV.*) The Lord is always caring for you, clearly showing you right from wrong and what He wants you to do.

84

Keep Drinking

Materials: Different assortment of pitchers

Scripture: *"But whosoever drinketh of the water that I shall give him shall never thirst; but the water that I shall give Him shall be in him a well of water springing up into everlasting life"* (John 4:14, KJV).

Who would like to hold these pitchers for me? (*Pass out the pitchers to the children.*) What does your mom make in your pitcher at home? (*Allow for answers.*) When you are really thirsty, what do you drink? (*Allow for answers.*)

Jesus says He will fill us up like a pitcher. But something is different when you have Jesus in your heart—you never run out. (*Read John 4:14, KJV.*) Do you think Jesus was really talking about water in this verse? (*No.*) He was saying that we can always depend on Him to love us and to care for our needs. We will never be alone again. We can come to Jesus again and again when we are in need. He will give us answers to our prayers. He will encourage us. He will love us and forgive our sins. And best of all, He is preparing a place for His children with Him in heaven. To be a child of God's, you must ask God to forgive your sins and invite Him into your heart. Then you will have everlasting life with Him. Jesus will keep filling up your life daily, just like the pitcher you are holding.

85

The Perfect Recipe

Materials: Mimeographed recipe for salvation, measuring cups, spoons, bowl.

Scripture: Take 1 generous cup of *forgiveness*.
(Ask the Lord to forgive your sins.)
"For all have sinned, and come short of the glory of God" (Rom. 3:23, KJV).

Blend 2 cups of *love*.
(Know that God loves you!)
"For God so loved the world, that he gave his only begotten Son, that whosoever believeth in him should not perish, but have everlasting life" (John 3:16, KJV).

Dust with 1 cup of *acceptance*.
(Ask Jesus to come into your heart and be your Savior.)
"Ask, and it shall be given you, seek, and ye shall find; knock and it shall be opened unto you. For every one that asketh receiveth; and he that seek-

eth findeth; and to him that knocketh it shall be opened" (Matt. 7:7-8, KJV).

Bake with *faith*.

I plan to use this recipe today. You help me read it, while I mix it together. First, I mix forgiveness. (*Allow one child to read part 1, while you pretend to mix.*) Then I add love. (*Allow another child to read part 2.*) Blend with acceptance. (*Allow a child to read part 3.*) And bake with faith.

All these things in our recipe add up to salvation. If you haven't received Christ as Savior yet, then study this recipe and I will be glad to pray with you after the service. You can be the most perfect recipe in the world.

86

A Perfect Fit

Materials: Forks, knives, spoons, and a silverware tray

Scripture: *"When someone becomes a Christian he becomes a brand new person inside. He is not the same any more. A new life has begun!"* (II Cor. 5:17, LB).

I have to put this silverware away. Will you help me? (*Pass some silverware out and allow the children to place it in the form fitting silverware tray.*) The silverware fits right into the spaces provided in this tray.

We should feel that way about new people who join our church. We don't all look the same on the outside. Some of us are forks, some are knives, and some are spoons. Yet, we should all fit in and find a place to serve the Lord together. Even though there are differences among us on the outside, we all have the spirit of the Lord on the inside. (*Read II Corinthians 5:17, LB.*)

Try to help people fit in when they become part of our church family. You will get a blessing by sharing and caring for others. Remember not to look on the *outside* appearance, but look on their hearts. Put all your love into this operation. It will make you and the new people happy.

87

Which Is Which?

Materials: A book that has a cover that looks like a Bible and a Bible. Cover titles with a piece of tape.

Scripture: *"All scripture is given by inspiration of God, and is profitable for doctrine, for reproof, for correction, for instruction in righteousness"* (II Tim. 3:16, KJV).

I'm holding two books here. They look alike. They have almost the same number of pages. Which one do you think is the real Bible? Hold your hands up if you think this one is the real Bible. Now, how many think this one is? It is hard to tell which book is the real Bible from the outside. How do you think we could tell? (*By reading what is inside*.) Yes, we must read what is on the inside.

The Bible was written over a span of two thousand years by over forty writers, but it was inspired by God and is the truth. (*Read II Timothy 3:16, KJV*.) God spoke to the writers and told them what to write down. So the Bible is the inspired Word of God, not just written by man.

Be careful what you read. Some people like to write things and pass them off as from the Lord. You can know the truth by comparing it with the Bible. If what you read agrees with the Bible, then it is truth.

88

Do You Get the Drift?

Materials: Talcum powder or baby powder, deodorant, perfume, after-shave lotion

Scripture: *"For we are unto God a sweet savour of Christ, in them that are saved, and in them that perish"* (II Cor. 2:15, KJV).

Today I brought some things from our medicine cabinet. Help me tell what they are. (*Name the items together.*) What do we use baby powder for? (*We put it on the baby as we diaper him to make him smell good.*) What do we use deodorant for? (*To keep us from having an odor from perspiration.*) What do ladies use perfume for? (*To smell good.*) Would anyone like to smell this one? (*Give children a turn to sniff the perfume.*) It smells good doesn't it? What do men use after-shave lotion for? (*To smell good.*) Do you like to be around a person who smells good? (*Yes.*)

God says that because Jesus is in our hearts, when we get saved, we are like a sweet smell. He likes to breathe deeply around His children, just to take in the delightful aroma. This expresses another way that God cares for us. Just as we try to put on pretty perfumes on the outside of our bodies to smell good, we should make our inside thoughts and actions sweet, too. Remember that this week. Try to be sweet on the inside as well as the outside.

89

The Search

Materials: A broom, coin, and candle, and someone to act out the parable of the lost coin

Scripture: *"Either what women having ten pieces of silver, if she lose one piece, doth not light a candle, and sweep the house, and seek diligently till she find it? And when she hath found it, she calleth her friends and her neighbors together, saying, Rejoice with me; for I have found the piece which I had lost. Likewise, I say unto you, there is a joy in the presence of the angels over one sinner that repenteth"* (Luke 15:8-10, KJV).

I'm going to read a story while my friend acts it out. (*Read Luke 15:8-10, KJV*.) (*Have a woman dressed like a Bible character act out the part of the woman and the lost coin*.)

Jesus was telling this story to the people to illustrate a point: each unsaved person is special to the kingdom of God. When a person accepts the Lord as Savior, the angels rejoice in heaven. Each person is the lost coin. Jesus is searching for him, like the woman searched for the coin. Even though there are already many saved people in His kingdom, Jesus still looks for the one who is not saved. God is not willing that any should perish. And when that one person asks the Lord into his heart, we all rejoice. If you haven't accepted the Lord, today is the day you can do it, and the angels will rejoice over you.

90

I Feel Wilted

Materials: One strong plant, one wilted or withered plant

Scripture: ". . . nourished up in the words of faith and of good doctrine, whereunto thou hast attained. But refuse profane and old wives' fables, and exercise thyself rather unto godliness. For bodily exercise profiteth little: but godliness is profitable unto all things, having promise of the life that now is, and of that which is to come" (I Tim. 4:6b-8, KJV).

I have two plants with me. Which one would you rather have? (*The living one!*) Why? (*It is going to produce or grow; it is pretty; etc.*) What do you think happened to the wilted plant? (*No water, poor soil, no sunshine, etc.*) You mean I should have watered this plant; and not have left it in the dark? I didn't know it needed water! I gave it spaghetti and meatballs—the same things I eat. No wonder it wilted.

The Bible says we need a special kind of nourishment to be a strong Christian. (*Read I Timothy 4:6b-8, KJV.*) We need good doctrine, godliness or godly exercise. Not all churches are giving good doctrine. In many cases, the ungodly members are very weak Christians, if they are even Christians at all. We need to nourish ourselves with the Bible and with clean thoughts, prayers, love, and care for others. This is spiritual exercise which helps us grow strong.

91

Pressed, Pleated, and Pleasing

Materials: Ironing board, iron, shirt to iron

Scripture: *"And he shall sit as a refiner and purifier of silver: and he shall purify the sons of Levi, and purge them as gold and silver, that they may offer unto the Lord an offering in righteousness"* (Mal. 3:3, KJV).

I've got a little experiment I want to try. Who would like to come up and press this wrinkled shirt? (*Allow for hands and choose one; have the child go over the wrinkled shirt without the iron turned on.*) Well, what's the matter here? I need that shirt ironed, but our iron isn't doing a very good job, is it? Set the iron up and see if it is hot. (*Allow child to touch cold iron, which is not turned on.*) Why won't this iron press out the wrinkles? (*It's not turned on.*) We need to have heat for the iron to do its job. Then it can press this shirt nice and smooth.

God often has to use a little heat on us to get our wrinkles out, too. There are sins that God has to spank us for—to help *straighten* us out. That way He smooths out our lives so that He can use us better. (*Read Malachi 3:3, KJV.*) God will make us righteous and better by applying a little heat to us when we need it.

92

Bend Over

Materials: Electric curlers, rollers, bobby pins, curling iron, chair

Scripture: *"And be not conformed to this world: but be ye transformed by the renewing of your mind, that ye may prove what is that good, and acceptable, and perfect, will of God"* (Rom. 12:2, KJV).

Today I am opening a beauty shop. Who would like to be my first customer? (*Allow for show of hands.*) I'm going to have this beauty shop for only a few minutes, so let's see what happens.

I brought all the right materials. Help me name what I have here. (*Hold up all items individually and allow children to name them.*) What do we use curlers for? (*To curl hair.*) I have to wind the hair around the curlers and leave them on for a while for them to mold the hair into a curly shape. (*Do this to a lock of hair on a child.*) We are changing the straight hair to curly hair. We are conforming it to the way we want it to shape. (*Have child return to seat.*)

God tells us to conform to Him and not to conform to the world. (*Read Romans 12:2, KJV.*) We should wrap ourselves around Christ and His principles, just as the hair is wrapped around the curlers. Then in a little while, we will be shaped like Christ.

93

Memories, Memories

Materials: A favorite scripture verse written by phrases on construction paper

Scripture: *"Thy word have I hid in my heart, that I might not sin against thee"* (Ps. 119:11, KJV).

How many of you have a good memory? Raise hands if you do. Okay, close your eyes. Someone tell me what color my shirt is. (*Allow for an answer.*) Open your eyes. (*Check to see if they are right.*) Close your eyes, and let's try it again. (*Children close their eyes.*) What do I have in my hand? (*Allow for an answer; Bible.*) Open your eyes and see. Yes, I do have a Bible. I guess you think you have pretty good minds. You are doing a great job of remembering.

Do you know that God wants us to do some memorizing? Here is a verse about learning to know God's Word by heart. (*Read Psalm 119:11, KJV.*) Let's see how long it takes us to memorize this verse. "*Thy word/ have I hid/ in my heart/ that I/ might not sin/ against thee*" Psalm 119:11.) We will go over it piece by piece. Some of you come up and hold these signs for me. (*Pick children to help.*) (*Go over this several times together.*) Do you think you know it by heart? Okay, let's put the signs down and say it without any cue cards. (*Try two times.*) Boy, you do know this verse! (*Have the sign holders mix positions.*) Okay, now we have to unscramble this puzzle. (*Do this together.*) I am very proud of this good memorizing job you have done. See how many other verses you can memorize this week.

94

The Light Dawns

Materials: A variety of lightbulbs, different shapes and sizes

Scripture: *"Thy word is a lamp unto my feet and a light unto my path"* (Ps. 119:105, KJV).

"And there will be no night there—no need for lamps or sun—for the Lord God will be their light; and they shall reign forever and ever" (Rev. 22:5, LB).

What are these little things I have with me today? (*Light bulbs*.) Would someone like to come up here and help me hold these light bulbs? (*Pick one child for each bulb*.) Now be real careful, because these are breakable. What do we use these bulbs for? (*Light*.) Some of them are used in special places. This one that looks like a flame belongs to our chandelier. The colored bulbs come from where? (*A Christmas tree*.) The regular light bulb belongs in our table lamp. The long bulb is fluorescent and is often in kitchens.

The Bible talks about lights in relation to God and His Word. The Bible is God's book to help us throughout our lives. Listen to this verse. (*Read Psalm 119:105, KJV*.) It says the Bible will direct our lives by lighting the way, like these light bulbs.

In another way the Bible talks about light. It says Jesus is the light of the world. Do you think we will need light bulbs in heaven? (*No*.) Because God will be there and light everything. Listen to Revelation 22:5 (LB). (*Read*.) God is so holy, pure, and magnificent that He will be the only light needed in heaven.

When you turn on and off the lights at home, remember that God and His Word are always there to guide you. He will light the path of your life and help you to live right.

95

Christi Is Like . . .

Materials: Construction paper, scissors, magic marker, glue, old magazines

Directions: Cut out magazine advertisements and glue one on each piece of construction paper. Print on the top "Christ is like . . ." On the back write the advertisement slogan. Example: Christ is like Coke. (On the back: He's the real thing.)

Kids, I want you to really think today. I guess some of you watch TV or see magazines. How many of you do? (*Raise hands.*) I want to see if you notice the commercials. I'm going to hold up a picture, and you tell me the commercial jingle or slogan that goes with it. Then we are going to apply it to Christ. Ready?

Christ is like Coke—He's the real thing.

Christ is like Kodak—He's a smile saver.

Christ is like Jello—There's always room for Him.

Christ is like Tide—He gets the stains out.

Christ is like Frosted Flakes—He's *great*!

You may add a lot more. We have had some fun relating Jesus to commercials. When you see a commercial, think how great God is. (*Sing chorus together.*)

Song: *"He's Everything to Me" (Ralph Carmichael)*

96

Brokenhearted
(*Valentine's Day*)

Materials: Flannelgraph board and an easel; ten red heart shapes cut into pieces (not too small), each piece with a strip of sandpaper glued on the back. (This will stick to the flannelgraph board.) Put each heart puzzle in separate envelopes so the pieces don't get mixed up. Allow children to assemble the broken hearts, one at a time.

Scripture: *"Those who sow tears shall reap joy"* (Ps. 126:5, LB).

"He heals the brokenhearted, binding up their wounds" (Ps. 147:3, LB).

Since it is close to Valentine's Day, I thought we would do some heart puzzles here on the flannelgraph board. Who would like to do the puzzle in envelope 1? (*Choose a helper, but be prepared to help if necessary. Continue doing heart puzzles as time permits.*) It is fun to put these broken hearts back together again. I like fixing things.

In real life, it is tough to be brokenhearted. But God can heal broken hearts. (*Read Psalm 147:3, LB.*) God loves us so much that He not only takes care of our physical hurts, but our emotional hurts as well. He cares for us when someone has treated us badly. (*Read Psalm 126:5, LB.*) That verse means you should care enough about someone to actually cry over their needs. Then when the needs are answered you will have great joy.

97

Heart Throb
(*Valentine's Day*)

Materials: Black, red, white, green, and gold construction paper cut in heart shapes.

Scripture: *"Blessed are they that keep his testimonies, and that seek him with the whole heart"* (Ps. 119:2, KJV).

Soon we will be celebrating Valentine's Day. What a day to share your feelings of love with someone! So today I brought some paper with which to tell a story. What shapes are these? (*Hold up hearts; allow for answer.*)

I need some helpers to hold up these hearts. (*Choose children to hold hearts. Pass out hearts in this order: black, red, white, green, and gold.*) I want to tell you about this first heart. It is black with sin, just like our hearts are before Christ comes in to be our Savior. Then our hearts are like this red heart; we have our sins covered and washed by the blood of Jesus. Third, our hearts are like this white heart; we have been scrubbed clean by Jesus. Then our hearts should become green. What do you think green represents? (*Growth.*) Yes, our lives should grow and mature in Christ. Finally, our hearts are like this gold heart. Our hearts are treasures, which we lay at the feet of God when we get to heaven. Let's review: black is a sinful heart; red is a heart washed with Jesus' blood; white is a clean, forgiven heart; green is a growing heart; and gold is a gift given to God.

98

Cluck, Cluck
(*Easter*)

Materials: A baby chick (Chicks can be bought at the dime store around the Easter holiday.)

Scripture: *"He will shield you with his wings! They will shelter you. His faithful promises are your armor"* (Ps. 91:4, LB).

"When you lie down, you will not be afraid; when you lie down your sleep will be sweet" (Prov. 3:24, NASB).

I want you to sit in a tight circle here on the floor where I placed newspapers. You may sit Indian style if it is comfortable for you. I brought a tiny, fuzzy baby with me today. I'm going to put it in the center of the circle so you can watch it while we talk. Try not to let him out of the circle. This baby chick is here just in time for the Easter holiday.

I want you to really listen. Have you ever watched a mother hen and her babies? When there is a storm, the mother hen gathers all her babies under her wings; she protects them. Our heavenly Father protects us by gathering us close to Him also. (*Read Psalm 91:4, LB.*) God does not want us to be fearful. Even when we are sleeping, God is watching over us. (*Read Proverbs 3:24, NASB.*) Just think, even when you are sleeping and your eyes are closed, God is watching over you. That is why the Bible says your sleep is sweet. This baby chick is loved and protected. And as a child of God, you are protected, too. What a wonderful blessing of love from God. (*Remember to take the chick and replace him in the box before the children get up, then remove him from the sanctuary.*)

99

Let Me Go!
(*Independence Day*)

Materials: Several lengths of rope with which to tie up some children, handcuffs with a key

Scripture: *"But now you are free from the power of sin and are slaves of God, and his benefits to you include holiness and everlasting life"*   (Rom. 6:22, LB).

"For the power of the lifegiving Spirit—and this power is mine through Jesus Christ—has freed me from the vicious circle of sin and death"   (Rom. 8:2, LB).

"The Lord is the Spirit who gives them life, and where he is there is freedom"   (II Cor. 3:17, LB).

I need some helpers today. (*Choose some children to tie up.*) I'm going to try an experiment. Put your hands together tight, while I tie them. (*Proceed to tie each child you choose.*) Now that you each are tied, how does it feel? It doesn't hurt yet, but how would you like to stay like that for a long time? It would hurt, wouldn't it? It's much better to be free, isn't it?

The only true freedom is when you are freed from sin. How can you be freed from the power of sin? (*By accepting Christ.*) Listen to what the Bible says about freedom from sin. (*Read Romans 6:22, LB; Romans 8:2, LB; and II Corinthians 3:17, LB.*) Each of you must choose Christ in order to be freed from sin. That doesn't mean you won't ever sin again. God no longer holds you accountable for the sins for which you ask forgiveness. You are free! Free from the bonds of sin and death. (*Untie the children.*)

100

I Am the Vine
(*Summer*)

Materials: A vine (watermelon, squash, cucumber, or cantaloupe)

Scripture: *"I am the true Vine, and my Father is the Gardener. He lops off every branch that doesn't produce. And he prunes those branches that bear fruit for even larger crops. He has already tended you by pruning you back for greater strength and usefulness by means of the commands I gave you. Take care to live in me, and let me live in you. For a branch can't produce fruit when severed from the vine. Nor can you be fruitful apart from me. Yes, I am the Vine; you are the branches. Whoever lives in me and I in him shall produce a large crop of fruit. For apart from me you can't do a thing"* (John 15:1-5, LB).

I brought a vine with me today. I picked this one out of the garden. It is a _____ (*insert the name*) vine. I expected it to grow _____ (*name the fruit expected*). Do you think it will still produce? (*No.*) Why not? (*It has been cut from the roots and rest of the vine.*) It cannot exist without being fed by the rest of the vine.

We are like that as Christians, too. We are part of God's family and we are fed by Him. (*Read John 15:1-5, LB.*) We must depend on God for knowledge and growth. God tends us and takes care of us. We can become useful through God. If we don't strive to grow, then God will prune (chop) off the dead, useless portions. Then we won't be dead weight to the rest of the vine.

Look closely at your Christian life. Are you growing and producing? Be a thriving, fruitful part of the Christian vine.

101

Pumpkin Flyers
(*Halloween*)

Materials: Orange construction paper, green yarn, hole punch

church name
location
service times
special up-coming events
Bible verse

Scripture: *"Therefore go and make disciples in all nations, baptizing them into the name of the Father and of the Son and of the Holy Spirit, and then teach these new disciples to obey all the commands I have given you; and be sure of this—that I am with you always, even to the end of the world"* (Matt. 28:19-20, LB).

It is going to be Halloween soon, and many of you are going to "trick or treat" this year. I have prepared some gifts for you to give to the people at the door.

Christ tells us in Matthew 28:19-20 that we should go to all the people all over the world and tell them about Him. Now maybe you are not ready to hop on a jet just yet to go to deepest Africa. But you have neighbors you will be seeing on Halloween night that you can witness to by giving them this pumpkin flyer.

On the flyer is a verse about Jesus and the times our church services begin. These people can come and hear more about Jesus. Even if they aren't home, you can hang this pumpkin flyer from the door knob, so they can find it when they come home. You will be a good messenger for Christ.

102

Halloween Fears

Materials: Several different Halloween masks—the scarier, the better

Scripture: *"The Lord is my light and my salvation; whom shall I fear?"* (Ps. 27:1, LB).

"For he orders his angels to protect you wherever you go" (Ps. 91:11, LB).

"That is why I am suffering here in jail and I am certainly not ashamed of it, for I know the one in whom I trust, and I am sure that He is able to safely guard all that I have given him until the day of his return" (II Tim. 1:12, LB).

I brought some scary masks with me today. It is close to Halloween and I thought you would like to try these on. Who would like to wear a mask for a little while? (*Choose as many helpers as you have masks.*)

What things scare you? (*Allow for a list of answers.*) Sometimes you feel afraid because you feel alone, but listen to Psalm 91:11, (LB). (*Read.*) God orders His angels to protect you wherever you are. What a wonderful promise. You do not need to be afraid with Jesus as your Savior. God also says in Psalm 27:1, (LB), that He is our light and salvation, and we don't have to be afraid of anything. These masks don't need to scare you at all. Neither do you need to fear the dark or thunder or anything. You have protection in Christ. That doesn't mean for us to be foolish and expect protection if we run out in front of a car—we would be hit. But it means we are protected from things which we don't control, such as storms or unseen fears.

103

Thank You Note (*Thanksgiving Day*)

Materials: A gift wrapped box, thank you note

Scripture: *"Let us come before his presence with thanksgiving, and make a joyful noise unto him with psalms"* (Ps. 95:2, KJV).

"Thanks be unto God for his unspeakable gift" (II Cor. 9:15, KJV).

I went to a birthday party last week and I took a present with me for the birthday boy. The present looked something like this. (*Hold up box.*) The birthday boy really liked his present, and several days later in the mail I received this thank you note. The note expressed how much he really appreciated my gift to him.

With Thanksgiving Day nearly here, I was reminded of our relationship with God. God gave us His Son as a present. Jesus sacrificed His life on the cross as a free gift of salvation. Have you ever written Jesus a thank you note for this tremendous gift? This gift is not a temporary thing. It is forever. This is the best gift ever, and yet some of us have never taken time to say thank you, as any polite recipient would.

I *really* want to take time this week to write a thank you note to Jesus. Until then, let's sing this chorus in closing:

Song: *Thank you Lord for saving my soul*
Thank you Lord for making me whole
Thank you Lord for giving to me
Thy great salvation so rich and free.

104

Chrismons (*Christmas*)

Materials: Glue, gold glitter, sheet of styrofoam or heavy white paper (12″ x 12″). Make one or two examples of these Chrismons ornaments. They are scriptural ornaments. Cut out the ornament, dip in glue, glitter in gold.

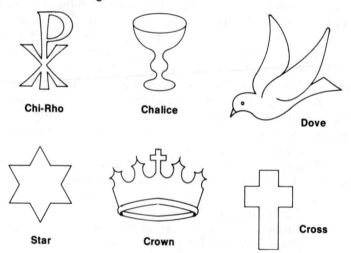

Chi-Rho

Chalice

Dove

Star

Crown

Cross

These ornaments are called Chrismons, because they are Christian ornaments. You can put these on your tree to remind you that Christmas is to celebrate Jesus' birth. They are made on white paper to show the purity and holiness of Christ. They can have gold glitter on them to show Christ's royalty.

I have a mimeographed sheet to give you with the patterns for the Chrismons. You can cut out the pattern and trace around it on white poster paper. Then glitter the edges, and hang the Chrismons on your tree with string.

The first Chrismon is Chi-Rho, Greek letters meaning Christ. The second is a chalice, or cup, Christ drank from. The third is the dove, a symbol of the Holy Spirit. The fourth is a star. The fifth is a crown. And the sixth is a cross. These Chrismons will remind you of Christ at Christmas. They represent things in the Bible.

The gold color represents the glory of God. Use white lights on your tree to show the power and holiness of God. The evergreen tree shows God's everlasting life. Wouldn't it be neat to have some special Christian Christmas ornaments that you can make?

Now help me explain these symbols: Chi-Rho are the letters in Christ's name (*show example*.) The chalice is what they drank from in the first what? (*Communion*.) (*Show example*.) What was shining over the city of Bethlehem? (*Star*.) What bird represents the Holy Spirit? (*Dove*.)

105

Star Bright
(*Christmas*)

Materials: Paper stars which can be pinned or taped to the children

Scripture: *"Let your light so shine before men, that they may see your good works, and glorify your Father which is in heaven"* (Matt. 5:16, KJV).

Do you remember what was up above Bethlehem in the sky on Christmas night? Yes, it was a star. But something was special about that star. What was it? Yes, it was the brightest of all the stars in the sky. But why was that star so bright? It was pointing out the place where Jesus was born.

The star is used as a decoration at Christmas to remind us of Christ's birth.

You are like a star, too, if you have given yourself to Christ. You should point people toward Christ. And the more you share about Christ, the more you grow in Christ. You shine inside, just like a star. People will notice your Christian love and caring. So, you can be just exactly like the star of Bethlehem. Remember to let your light shine, just like Matthew 5:16 says. (*Read Matthew 5:16*.) Each day you will glorify God. Here is a star to pin on to remind you to shine.

106

Christmas Cross

Materials: Scissors, multi-colored construction paper, wrapping bows, magic marker.

Construct:

1. A cross out of green paper about 5' x 3'. Put a star at the top and tape cross to the pulpit or front wall. Print on the horizontal "God's Gift—Jesus' Life"

2. Attach a bow to 12" x 8" piece of construction paper, and print on it "Our Gifts to God" as the children tell you what they would like to give God. Tape this beneath the Christmas cross.

Scripture: *"For when we were yet without strength, in due time Christ died for the ungodly. For scarcely for a righteous man will one die: yet peradventure for a good man some would even dare to die. But God commendeth his love toward us, in that, while we were yet sinners, Christ died for us"* (Rom. 5:6-8, KJV).

I taped up in front (*point out*) a Christmas cross. During this time of year we have Christmas trees, but I thought we would look at the real purpose of baby Jesus being born at this time. What color is the Christmas cross? (*Green.*) This shows us that God is everlasting. Christ died for all our sins. (*Read Romans 5:6-8, KJV.*)

What do you see at the top of the Christmas cross? (*Star.*) This means Jesus was special. He was *not* just any ordinary man being crucified. He is *God's Son*. God gave us a very precious gift through the birth of baby Jesus. God gave us a way to get rid of our sins and enter into heaven for eternity. God gave us His *only* Son. That is the best gift we will ever receive.

Let's list some small gifts we can give back to God (*Allow children's answers: hard work, prayer, clean tongue, control of our tempers, etc.*) I will write your answers on this present and place it beneath the cross. While we can never match God's gift, that of Jesus' life, we can express our love to Him by doing these good things. Ask God to help you work hard at keeping these promises.